The Mysteries
Meet the Mysteries of the Sky

"Like my predecessor Dr. Chopra, I believe that the ancient arts and practices of medicine still have much to teach about ourselves and our understanding of illness. Astrology had been taught for centuries as an integral part of a physician's training. However, with the advent of the industrial revolution and the rise of science, many of the old teachings were abandoned. With the recent explosion of interest in alternative health techniques and ancient medical practices, medical schools are once again starting to teach a new generation of doctors the old ways."

— Mitchell E. Gibson, M.D.

- Learn to detect depression, anxiety, addictive disorder, schizophrenia, and attention deficit hyperactivity disorder in a client's chart
- See the astrological markers for mental illness in the charts of Princess Diana, Marshall Applewhite, Charles Dickens, Mike Wallace and others
- Learn the basics of astrology if you are new to the science

About the Author

Dr. Mitchell E. Gibson, twice named to the Woodward and White listing of the "Best Doctors in America," is a practicing psychiatrist and one of the most well-known and highly respected medical doctors in the state of Arizona. He is a diplomate of the American Board of Psychology and Neurology, the American College of Forensic Medicine, and the American Board of Forensic Examiners. Dr. Gibson is former Chief of Staff of the East Valley Camelback Hospital and was Chief Resident in Psychiatry at the Albert Einstein Medical Center in Philadelphia. He is a highly-sought mental health consultant to television, radio, and print media services and Fortune 500 companies, and has spoken at numerous professional conventions.

Dr. Gibson is a Research Member of the American Federation of Astrologers and writes regular feature articles for their monthly journal. In addition to his other accomplishments, Dr. Gibson is an accomplished contemporary artist and has displayed his works in New York, Los Angeles, Paris, and numerous other cities around the globe. He recently received the Jury Prize for Creativity in a competition at the Museum of Fine Art in Paris, and his work is published in the *Encyclopedia of Living Artists* and *New Art International*.

To Contact the Author

If you would like to contact the author or would like more information about this book, please write in care of Llewellyn Worldwide. All mail addressed to the author is forwarded, but the publisher cannot, unless specifically instructed by the author, give out an address or phone number. Please write to:

Dr. Mitchell Gibson
c/o Llewellyn Publications
P.O. Box 64383, Dept. K302–6
St. Paul, MN 55164-0383, U.S.A

Please enclose a self-addressed, stamped envelope for reply or $1.00 to cover costs. If ordering from outside the U.S.A., please enclose an international postal reply coupon.

SIGNS

of
mental
illness

Mitchell E. Gibson, M.D.

1999
Llewellyn Publications
St. Paul, MN 55164-0383 U.S.A.

FIRST EDITION
Second Printing, 1999

Cover design: Tom Grewe
Cover photo: Still/n/Motion (Phoenix, AZ)
Editing and book design: Ken Schubert

Library of Congress Cataloging-in-Publication Data

Gibson, Mitchell E., 1959–
    Signs of mental illness : an astrological and psychiatric
breakthrough / Mitchell E. Gibson. -- 1st ed.
        p. cm.
    Includes bibliographical references.
    ISBN 1-56718-302-6 (pbk.)
    1. Astrology and mental illness.   I. Title.
BF1729.M452G53   1998
133.5--dc21   98-20176
                                                                CIP

Publisher's Notes

The information in this book is for educational purposes only, and should not be construed as a substitute for or alternative to professional medical and/or psychiatric diagnosis.
Llewellyn Worldwide does not participate in, endorse, or have any authority or responsibility concerning private business transactions between our authors and the public.
All mail addressed to the author will be forwarded but the publisher cannot, unless specifically instructed by the author, give out an address or phone number.

Printed in the United States of America

Llewellyn Publications
A Division of Llewellyn Worldwide, Ltd.
P.O. Box 64383, Dept. K302-6
St. Paul, MN 55164-0383, U.S.A.

Contents

Acknowledgements

I would like to thank all of the people who have helped to make this project possible:

Noel Tyl for his vision, guidance, and understanding, Carl Llewellyn Weschcke for believing in me, Sharon Mattingly my office manager for putting up with my moods during the time that I wrote this, Ms. Kamau Ramsey for her kind advice and spirit, Dr. Andy Hogg for his encouragement, Lois Rodden for all of her excellent data and time, Janice Thomas for her wonderfully kind and funny e-mails, Barbara Wilson for her patience and friendship, to Thoth for his inspiring dreams, Dr. Tali Arik for that sanity restoring trip to Las Vegas, Beverly Torres (my dear sister) who never stopped believing in me, and most of all to all of my dear friends and family who endured my extended periods of solitude and research over the past year.

Nature is man's teacher. She unfolds her treasures to his search, unseals his eye, illumines his mind, and purifies his heart; an influence breathes from all the sights and sounds of her existence.

— Alfred Billings Street

Introduction

IF SOMEONE HAD TOLD ME WHILE I WAS IN MEDICAL SCHOOL THAT I would someday write a book on the correlations between psychiatry and astrology, I would have laughed long and hard at them. After that, I would have suggested that they see a good counselor for several dozen sobering therapy sessions. Such was my opinion of the entire genre of psychics, astrologers, clairvoyants, and anyone even remotely connected to the area of the paranormal. What I did not know was that the universe had a whole litany of surprises in store for this unsuspecting medical student!

I graduated from UNC Chapel Hill in the spring of 1985 and decided to pursue a residency program in psychiatry at the Albert Einstein Medical Center in Philadelphia. My girlfriend (who was later to become my first wife) was heavily interested in mysticism, healing, and astrology.

One day, she went to see an astrologer in town. She returned claiming that he was the best astrologer that she had ever met, and that she thought he and I would get along well. With some trepidation (and more than a little arm twisting) I made an appointment to see him.

I expected to meet an old man with a Merlinesque demeanor surrounded by cats in a darkened old house cluttered by an odd variety of crystals, wide-eyed statues, and other things that looked as if they could go bump in the night. I was not to be disappointed. Dr. Jacob Schwartz was just such a man.

That meeting changed my entire life. Armed with only the date, place, and time of my birth, Dr. Schwartz proceeded to tell me exceedingly detailed facts about my life, aspirations, dreams, and a certain mechanical problem with my car that materialized approximately when he said it would. He was very methodical and scientific in his presentation, something I did not expect from a man who spent a good bit of time keeping his cats away from his charts. He told me the month and day that my parents had separated and the astrological correlates for why it had happened at that time. He told me about my profession and why I chose it. He also told me what I really wanted to do with my life and why. He was highly accurate on both counts.

Prior to that first meeting, all he knew of me was my birth data. As he talked and explained his technique and reasoning, I began to understand that I was being shown an art that was well developed, sound in its principles, and obviously quite useful. As a psychiatrist, I knew that I could never glean that kind of detailed information about a person's life from simply knowing their birth data and shaking their hand. Quite simply, I began to realize that Dr. Schwartz was better at what he did than I was at what I did! That thought was intensely unsettling to me. I must have listened to his tape thirty times before I accepted that fact. I could only bring myself to see him once, but that one visit was enough. I had been initiated into an ancient art.

I began an exhaustive study of astrology, and for the next ten years I ran thousands of charts of friends, family, patients, colleagues, and anyone else who would sit still for a reading. I studied the works of Carl Jung, who at the time was the only other psychiatrist I was aware of that had taken an active interest in this ancient art. I studied classical astrology from the Greek, Roman, Mayan, Egyptian, Chinese, and Babylonian cultures. What I gradually and painfully began to realize was that modern science had emerged from an admixture of alchemy and astrology. I also realized that at one time in the not-too-distant past, astrology and medicine were inextricably linked in a sort of primeval dance that held a deep and hidden link to the inner nature of humanity. At one time, all medical doctors were trained in astrology. Indeed, any doctor who was not a competent astrologer was considered to be a charlatan!

Such is not the case in today's world. Today, medical doctors are besieged from many sides including the public, lawyers, insurance companies, the media, and a host of other parties who are trying to shape and mold the future of modern medicine. However, any discipline that is to survive must somehow come to terms with its origins. Medicine is now being forced to acknowledge the usefulness and veracity of ancient and alternative methods of healing. Among these are homeopathy, herbology, acupuncture, crystals, and a host of other disciplines that, ten years ago, no self-respecting doctor who valued his license would admit to having any knowledge of. As I have followed these dizzying changes in medicine, I often return to that long afternoon that I spent with Dr. Schwartz, and a nagging question plagues my waking thoughts: are we destined by some monstrously complex series of "plans" to have certain life patterns?

For centuries, astrologers have looked to the stars for guidance and direction in their own lives and the lives of their clients. Adolph Hitler used the most brilliant astrologers and psychics in all of Germany to help him plan the strategies that almost won him the war. It is said that one of his astrologers was so adept in the art that he could accurately predict who would call the Führer and at precisely what time the phone would ring!

Such was the respect of the Allied forces for the talents of the Nazi paranormal cadre that they soon formed their own secret team of occult specialists to counter them. One of the most famous of these was a British unit known as MI5, which was composed in part of some very talented astrologers. Each move calculated by Hitler's astrologers to give the Nazis a battle advantage was countered by the Allied astrologers. At one time during the war, Hitler dropped leaflets over Europe containing quatrains of Nostradamus which supposedly "predicted" his eventual victory in the war. Not to be outdone, Allied bombers subsequently dropped different quatrains which showed that Hitler (Hister) was destined to go down in defeat. Nostradamus had made his predictions using astrology.

Linus Pauling and Carl Jung once collaborated on a research project designed to study the phenomenon of synchronicity. At the end of the project they came to a conclusion they believed to be inescapable. These two great minds came to believe that all events that happened in our universe were guided by an ordering intelligence.

If there is an "ordering intelligence" in the world and if the concept of predestination is a valid one, then there should be valid "signs" at the start of any event which point to the possible future course of that event. In the following work, I have applied this reasoning to a search for the astrological signs that might suggest a possible future that includes mental illness. I believe that it is possible to show consistent planetary configurations present at the time of a person's birth that suggest the presence of mental health or illness.

All the patients in this study have been diagnosed according to the gold standard of psychiatric diagnosis: DSM-IV (*Diagnostic and Statistical Manual, Volume 4*). They were chosen because they represent the most common causes of human mental and emotional suffering: Major Depression, Anxiety Disorder, Addictive Disorder, Schizophrenia, and Attention Deficit Hyperactivity Disorder (ADHD).

I invite the reader to take a journey into the unknown, to an area of astrological data never before explored. I present to you *Signs of Mental Illness*.

1   Facts and Fictions

IN EVALUATING ASTROLOGY, IT IS ALWAYS NECESSARY TO DISTINGUISH between its simplistic popular literature and the student's rules of chart construction and interpretation. In the first case, we have Sun-sign or newspaper astrology with its single variable of twelve zodiacal divisions. In the second, we have the actual casting of a horoscope, which involves dozens of variables and utilizes intervals of a few minutes (and occasionally a few seconds) of birth time for the purpose of interpretation. In terms of method, the difference between these two is equivalent to utilizing 2% versus 85% of one's subject data, and what goes into a method is reflected in what comes out of it. In other words, only a discrete natal chart can be the basis of serious results, and its provision that almost everyone in the world has distinct life probabilities is astrology's own answer to Sun-signing, with its mere twelve options for the whole of humankind.

The problems we find in "real" astrology are, by contrast, due to its abundance of data and almost inexhaustible imposition of definitions. A horoscope is a diagram of the position of the Sun, Moon, planets, lunar nodes and ascendant, as well as the major angular relationships, or *aspects,* between them, cast for a particular moment and location. Each variable occupies one of twelve signs as well as one of twelve houses. Consequently, every variable (except the ascendant) has 144 possibilities, and, in aspect with any other variable, 20,736 possibilities, each with its individual significance. In all, aspect possibilities number over two million— and this is without considering them in combination, or observing house cusps, zodiacal degrees, soli-lunar pairing, declinational positions, or other defining factors.

I very much doubt whether any astrologer in the world has a mental concept corresponding to all of these aspects. But a good astrologer will know the more important ones, and, with a well-honed intuition, can combine the individual principles of sign, house, and aspect in a meaningful way.

The experienced astrologer understands the limitations of books, and uses them more for annotations than as guides. Of necessity, astrological textbooks or computer programs treat each principle individually, and so are either too limited or too generalized in their statements to provide more than a basic foundation of astrological understanding. It is the skillful analysis and synthesis of a horoscope that is the mark of a real astrologer.

But the "instant adept" who takes a half-dozen lessons and then hangs out a shingle can be an embarrassment when they go public. I recall one in particular who, in the hope of winning a large cash prize, tried his hand at identifying the Sun signs of individuals from their physical appearance. He failed with distinction, as any real astrologer would have predicted, but the episode is still replayed on television, and cited as an argument against astrology.

MAKING THE CASE

Yet some very capable astrologers have also been tested publicly, and with quite different results (though their successes are much less publicized). One example is Sydney Omarr, whose astrological expertise was utilized by the Allied Forces (U.S. Army Intelligence) during World War II. Challenged over the radio to calculate the vocation of an unknown critic, Omarr then and there set up a chart and correctly identified her as a psychologist.

Similarly, astrologer Evangeline Adams (J. P. Morgan's astrological counselor) described, from a natal chart, the daughter of the judge presiding at her trial in great detail. Adams had been brought into court under an old fortune-telling law, and Judge Freschi, not knowing how else to decide the case, gave her the birth data and requested a reading. Adams wasn't given the subject's name, but her remarks so impressed the judge that he dismissed the charge against her and declared in his closing remarks that "Adams raises the dignity of astrology to an exact science."

The great astronomer Johannes Kepler once gained royal patronage on the basis of a horoscope he had drawn of someone unknown to him. Such examples, taken from the public record, could be multiplied many times over, and it is good to remember this when we read critics like the late Carl Sagan who insisted that no astrologer can say anything meaningful about an individual he has not seen. The truth is that every competent astrologer can do this.

Critics of astrology are quick to condemn it as a pseudo-science and superstition. But in that case, what are we to make of the truly great minds who were lifelong students and proponents of astrology? How are we to explain Newton's unequivocal defense of the subject, and his terse dismissal of those who condemn astrology without studying it or testing its validity? How are we to account for the more than 800 horoscopes drawn up by Kepler, and the conspicuous success of his published predictions of weather patterns, wars and uprisings?

Carl Sagan attempted to disarm these facts by painting a neurotic picture of Newton and explaining Kepler's astrologizing in terms of economic pressures. But what is the relevance of these things? Why should Newton's introversion or Kepler's desire for material security prejudice the validity of their astrological studies any more than it does their physics and astronomy? This is the logic of innuendo, and it wears increasingly thin as other partisans are added to the list. For example, what eccentricity required the pioneer psychiatrist Carl Jung to study astrology and use it in his research?

SCIENCE OR NOT?

Of course, astrology is not a science in the usual sense. Not only are most of its variables mathematical only, but its logic is qualitative and even analogous. This, however, merely raises questions of classification. Validity is a matter of testing, and in this regard, astrology can be measured by the same statistical laws that apply to any other predictive system.

Again, though astrology is a probabilistic rather than deterministic tool, though it concedes the modifying power of both the human and divine will, and even allows for the existence of two uncharted, transplutonian planets, it can still, in competent hands, exceed any semblance of chance expectations in a number of important areas. That such data continues to be denied a public hearing is no slur on astrology, but rather on the critics, who have typically refused either to study the subject or examine the results of those who have.

THEORETICAL ARGUMENTS

The most frequent objection to astrology is that the distance of the planets is too great for them to exert their alleged influences. Granting the physical facts, what is it exactly that astrology does allege? I have already pointed out that most of its variables are mathematical only, and have no physical correlate on the celestial sphere. And since these impact precisely as do the physical Sun, Moon, and planets, both in their aspects and transits, there is no reason to infer a material involvement anywhere in the astrological system. It may be that astrological influences are occult, or even karmic, and that the synchronicity of the orbital positions merely serves to define and clock the effects. Either way, however, physical distance is not a factor, so an objection based on physical distance is not relevant.

It is also argued that Western astrology does not take into consideration the precession of the poles. This is perfectly true, but again entirely irrelevant since the Western system does not chart by the stars, but by the fixed point of the vernal equinox.

Then there is the "twins" argument. If astrology is true, shouldn't twins follow the same or very similar life patterns? The answer is that some of them—the twins with nearly identical horoscopes—do just this. In the case of celebrated "Jim twins," separated almost from birth and reunited in middle age, each individual had received the same adoptive name, had an adoptive brother of the same name, had married twice to women of the same names, had given the same names each to their son and dog (in the case of the son, both first and middle names), had followed identical careers, had identical hobbies and health patterns, and preferred the same brands of cars, cigarettes and beer. Another pair of "exact" twins attended medical school together, set up a joint practice, simultaneously succumbed to drug addiction, and died together in a suicide pact.

The lives of twins diverge in the same respects that their charts do. There is no fixed rule, it is simply a question of where things happen to fall. In some instances, a difference of less than a minute of birth time can work a profound change, while in others, ten or fifteen minutes may not do so. Again, where the charts of twins share adverse social aspects, it will create a disharmony between them, and this can exaggerate their differences in some startling ways.

I recall an example of this from central Florida, about a decade ago. The twins (male) in this case were inseparable as children, and afterwards worked together, first as acrobats, and then in running an auto service shop. Both were outgoing and aggressive, but in the one I call Twin B, these traits were strongly magnified, leading to increased friction between them. Twin B then developed criminal contacts and proclivities, and became a partner in an auto theft ring. He was arrested first for theft, and then for arson and assault. While awaiting trial for these charges, he conspired with one of his partners to murder another partner. One one of the more sensational aspects of the trial was that crucial testimony leading to the conviction of Twin B was provided by his brother.

Cases of this sort demonstrate the astrological complexity of twinning and the dramatic contrast that can result, under certain circumstances, from even small differences in birth time. Most of these studies have been confined to biological pairs, but much more could be learned if they were extended to all astrological "twins," defined as any two people with identical birth charts.

BIBLICAL INJUNCTIONS

Lastly, we have the so-called religious objection to astrology. Of course, this does not really have anything to do with religion, or, for that matter, with morals, but is based entirely on the interdiction of Old Testament prophets, who identified astrology with the Babylonians and Egyptians, their abhorred captors. Not many Jews today maintain this historical bias any more than they reject art because of the Mosaic injunction against graven images. Ironically, however, the fundamentalist (Bible literalist) Christians, who have no Jewish obligations, and for whom the Old Testament should be mere prologue, have resurrected this old antipathy, which they now wave like an *oriflamme* of universal law. Thus, Jerry Falwell tells us that a belief in astrology is incompatible with a belief in God, while some would even extend that belief to say that astrology is a black art. Of course, this is the same mentality that gets frothy when exposed to evolutionary or geological science, and is now actively engaged in banning children's books like *The Wizard of Oz*. Until recently, it still argued that the Earth is flat and fixed in the center of the universe.

There are hundreds of associations and references to astrology in the Bible. In *Ezekiel* 4:6, God says: "I have appointed thee each day for a year." Astrologers use this statement in calculating progressions, and it works. In *Job* 38:32, there is a reference to the word *Mazzaroth*. This word means "signs of the Zodiac." *Ecclesiastes* 3:1–8 states: "To every thing there is a season, and a time to every purpose under the heaven: a time be born, and a time to die; a time to plant, and a time to pluck up that which is planted; a time to kill, and a time to heal; a time to break down, and a time to build up; a time to get, and a time to lose; a time to keep and a time to cast away; a time to love, a time to hate." Astrologers are very firm in their belief that there is indeed a right and a wrong time to do everything!

The Catholic Church, despite its own resistance to modern science, has never shared this particular prejudice, and many of its popes and monks have actually been serious astrologers. In fact, Western astrology would not now be the tool it is but for the Spanish monk Placidus de Titus, who successfully worked out the complex geometry of house construction from a bewildering maze of theoretical possibilities.

ALLOWING THE POSSIBILITIES

Because they refuse to examine it, few scientists today appreciate the niceties of spherical astronomy that have gone into the development of the Placidian chart. I suppose it is largely a fear that astrology kicks out the foundations of their world view that breeds an *a priori* defensiveness towards it. But scientists, if anyone, should proceed without prejudice in any investigation. Those who take the trouble to test astrology properly are rarely prepared for its often startling results.

It is true, of course, that no causal process can exist in a vacuum, and that if astrology is valid, our world view must differ in some respects from what we now imagine. But different is not necessarily contradictory. Astrology, as a cyclical concept, can be perfectly well understood by an extension of the quantitative logic that now governs our sciences. I believe, for example, that there are more than enough probabilities in genetic transmission to accommodate the laws of astrology. It is only because we truncate our logic and do not allow it to follow our total life experience into the *qualitative* realms that metaphysical realities seem bizarre and unbelievable to many.

This fact does not, however, deter a long succession of heads of state, presidents and their first ladies, and a large number of Fortune 500 company executives from retaining astrologers on their payrolls.

2   Astrology and Medicine

MODERN MEDICAL TRAINING RELIES HEAVILY ON THE LATEST TECHNO-
logical advances in order to prepare medical students for their
future practices. Typically, this training includes the study of surgery,
pharmacology, pediatrics, geriatrics, anatomy, microbiology, and a
host of other equally complex and challenging courses. However,
most medical doctors do not realize that these are only recent addi-
tions in their training curricula. There was a time in the not-too-distant past that doctors were also taught herbology, leeching, humor
theory, and astrology. Indeed, astrology has been practiced as an
integral part of medicine for more than 2,000 years. For centuries,
many of humanity's greatest thinkers have explored the relationship
between medicine and astrology. In this chapter, I will review this
fascinating and largely untold historical connection.

ANCIENT WISDOM

Empedocles (490–430 B.C.), a early Greek philosopher and physician, drew from the work of Hermes Trismegistus and the cosmol-
ogy of Egypt. He taught that all life was derived from the four elements—fire, air, earth, and water—and that out of imbalances of
these various mixtures arose all disease. The principle of the four
elements has been utilized extensively throughout astrology.

On the island of Cos in the Aegean Sea was a shrine to Aes-
culapius, the God of healing. It was here that Hippocrates
(460–377 B.C.), the most famous physician of all time, was born.
Hippocrates worked out a system in which each part of the
human body was correlated with either a fixed star or a planet.

Aristotle (384–322 B.C.), famed son of court physician Nichomachus, was the most gifted of Plato's students and tutor to the young prince who was to become Alexander the Great. He created an astrological picture of the world and ascribed disease to a faulty mixture of the body's *humors* (his interpretation of the action of the four elements on the human body). His teachings on astrology, humoral medicine, and disease were to be required learning for centuries to come in all European medical schools.

C. Plinius Secundus (A.D. 23–79) wrote an encyclopedia under the title *Naturalis Historia* (Natural History) that contained information on astrological medicine.

Krinas of Messalia (circa A.D. 60), an astrologer and physician, practiced in Rome in the time of Nero. He treated his patients according to the current positions of the planets.

Ptolemy (A.D. 100–178), mathematician, astronomer, astrologer, and physician, was one of the greatest scientists of antiquity. He incorporated the investigations of earlier scientists into his works. He is generally acknowledged as one of the greatest astrologers who ever lived. His great work *Tetrabiblos* is still in print. In it, he postulates extensively about planetary diseases, writing that Saturn "induces general disorders and chronic diseases in the human body," and that Mars has an affinity with painful disease and excessive infant mortality. His work is a great inspiration to my understanding of the principles of astromedicine.

Galen (A.D. 129–200) was the most famous medical practitioner of imperial Rome and was the personal physician to Emperor Marcus Aurelius. He elaborated on the theory of the elements and humors in his writings and practice.

MIDDLE AGES

After the classical world had passed, the Arabs became the chief practitioners of astrology, which to this day plays an exceedingly important part in the daily life of Moslem nations.

As trade was established with the Arabs, the doctrine of astrology penetrated into medieval Europe, which proved fertile ground for its growth. Kings, emperors, princes, and rulers of the church all had implicit faith in the influence of the stars, and there were few who did not retain astrologers to advise and forewarn them.

Not only was astrology the ardent study of the most learned and powerful minds, but among the masses of the people its authority and guidance were accepted without question. It was common for a large sum to be paid for the erection of a horoscope, which would be consulted at every important period of the owner's life. This practice is continued today in Fortune 500 companies, Hollywood studios, and even the White House!

Astrology and medicine were so tightly linked during the Middle Ages that Theophrastus Bombastus Von Hohnheim (Paracelsus, 1493–1541), an extremely prominent physician, philosopher, and astrologer, expressed the opinion that a doctor with no astrological knowledge was a "pseudomedicus" (a sham doctor)!

One of the most famous physicians of all time was also a legendary astrologer: Michelle de Nostradame (Nostradamus, 1503–1566). His medical treatments for the plague made him famous throughout all of Europe. His primary claim to fame continues to be his quatrains which incorporated his vast knowledge of astrology, philosophy, and the occult into an uncanny ability to foresee the future. He is truly one of the enigmatic figures of all time.

Francis Bacon (1562–1656) considered that astrology was useful in weather forecasting and for agriculture and that it was invaluable in questions of health.

Robert Fludd (1571–1630), physician, astrologer, and Rosicrucian, described how the interplay of macrocosmic (stellar) forces and microcosmic (biological) forces combined to strongly influence the pattern of all life on Earth.

Many of the eminent astrologers of those times are famous today for their achievements in other sciences. They include such celebrated scholars as Regiomontanus, Bishop of Ratisbon, who reformed the calendar; Johannes Kepler, who discovered the fundamental laws on which the solar system is built; Tycho Brahe, the great Danish astronomer; Jerome Cardan, physician, philosopher and mystic; Pierre Gassendi, one of the world's greatest mathematicians; Philip Melancthon, pioneer of the reformation; and John Flamsteed, astronomer royal of England.

The list of history's prominent astrologers reads like a *Who's Who* of the academic and medical world of the past. From this brief sampling, there can be little doubt that astrology held a lofty place in the intellectual world of the Middle Ages.

MODERN ADVANCES

The period from the eighteenth century to modern times has ushered in a vastly different view of astrology than that of the ancients. The modern emphasis on empirical reasoning and mechanism has contributed to the demise of the public study of astrology by most scientists. However, a surprising number of researchers continue to labor untiringly at uncovering the secret connections between astrology and medicine. Most of these scientists are not generally well known outside of their own circle of colleagues, but their research is important in continuing the ancient tradition of study begun by the great master scientists of the past.

In the early 1900s, Alex Bethor launched a periodical titled *Zodiacus*. The *Astrologische Rundshau* (The Astrological Review), and the *Astrologischen Blätter* (Astrological Papers) soon followed. Each of these periodicals regularly included articles on the connection between disease and astrological influences.

In 1914, Dr. Friedrich Feerhow's *Die mediainishe Astrologie* was published, in which he claims to be the first person to attempt to find a scientific causal explanation of the connection between astrology and health. In this work, Dr. Feerhow presents many chart examples of patients, along with references to other pioneering astro-medical researchers.

In 1926, Baron. Herbert von Klöckler (who was a physician) published *Astrologie als Erfahrungsweissenschaft*, in which he first presented the use of statistics to legitimize the findings of astrology.

In 1927, Dr. Karl Bayer produced his dissertation, *Die Grundprobleme der Astrologie* (The Fundamental Problems of Astrology), in which he said that it is possible for astrology to fulfill all the requirements of a science. Bayer saw astrology's role as filling the gap between physical science and psychology.

In 1928, Dr. Olga Friefau studied astrology's relation to medicine and psychotherapy. In her 1928 book *Die innerseelische Erfahrungswelt am Bilde der Astrologie* (The World of Inner Experience as Represented by Astrology), she brought together the vocabularies and correspondences of astrology and psychology.

In 1949, the first congress for Cosmobiological Research was held at Aalen. This has now become an annual event.

In 1974, Dr. Agoston Terres discovered that the positions of the planets cause variations in the Earth's magnetic field. He also showed that these variations are statistically related to disease symptoms, crimes, and other phenomena.

In 1973, Dr. Michel Gauqelin published his now-legendary work *Cosmic Influences On Human Behavior*. This well-written and well-researched book has been accepted internationally as the first serious attempt by a medical researcher to relate vocation to the birth horoscope. In studying the births of 25,000 European professionals listed in *Who's Who,* Dr. Gauqelin discovered that certain planets were found more frequently at the rising or culminating positions in the horoscope. For example, Mars ascended or culminated in the case of athletes with the probability against chance distribution ranging from one in 50,000 to one in 1,000,000! When first published, this was hailed as the most important scientific backing that astrology ever received. From a strictly scientific viewpoint, Dr. Gauquelin validated the astrological hypothesis: the existence of a correlation between the state of the solar system and human experience.

THE CURRENT SITUATION

In most modern countries, medicine and astrology are not connected in any formal way. Most Western medical scientists consider astrology to be an outdated pseudoscience that has little or no place in the halls of academia.

However, in modern Tibet, medicine and astrology are still taught in conjunction with each other. Astrology students there are not required to study medicine, but medical students are required to study astrology. Tibetan horoscopes chart the unfolding of a person's life, unlike their European counterparts, which describe the personality based on the natal situation. Physicians consult medical astrology when determining the best day to apply the many kinds of treatments. The patient's life-force and life-spirit days are determined from their natal animal signs.

Most Tibetans wish to know the time of their death so that they can prepare for a good rebirth. However, they also believe that even though a person's life span can be calculated, it can be extended with prayer and good deeds, or shortened by such events as earthquake, war, or a terminal illness if one does not have the karmic potential to survive such events. The Tibetan word for star is *karma*. Tibetan doctors believe that one's karma is written in the stars.

Now that Pluto has entered Sagittarius, the acceptance of astrology and other "New Age" sciences will begin to occur at a faster pace. Already, the tacit acceptance of angels, UFOs, and paranormal phenomena is starting to come forth into mainstream consciousness. As we approach a new millennium, perhaps today's greatest minds will understand the importance of completing the great work of exploring our relationship to the cosmos. In addition, Western society may also begin to appreciate our unique relationship to the stars and planets from a deeper and more enlightened perspective.

3   The Basics of Astrology

MANY OF THE PEOPLE READING THIS BOOK WILL NOT HAVE A WORK-
ing knowledge of astrology and its basic principles, so this chapter
will provide a brief introduction in the hope of making the terms
used in the main body of the research more easily comprehensible.

THE PLANETS

The zodiac and its associated myths are of essential value in
astrology. This band of twelve "signs" represents the positions the
planets occupy along the ecliptic as seen from Earth, and greatly
influences astrological interpretation and prediction. Each planet
is given a special relationship with a sign of the zodiac.

Each of the planets and signs are associated with positive and
negative traits, called *dignities*, that help shape the course of a particular reading. A planet increases in power when it is in its home
or *ruling sign*. In the classical system, the Sun and Moon rule one
sign each, and the other planets two signs each. (Astrologers, for
the sake of convenience, usually refer to the Sun and Moon as
planets.) A planet in *exaltation* is well placed and should posi-
tively influence a person's life. A planet in *detriment* is ill-placed
and loses some of its power. A planet in *fall* is at its weakest.

☉ The Sun

The Sun is the most prominent heavenly body in the solar system.
It is the star around which Earth and the rest of the planets orbit.

In Western astrology, the Sun is associated with the gods Ra
and Apollo. In Mesopotamian astrology, the Sun god was

Shamash (Utu), who represented the life-giving rays of the Sun. He was an all-seeing god who was also the god of justice, protecting good and destroying evil.

In the birth chart, the Sun is the basic self and its position within a particular sign colors the entire orientation of the personality. The aspects made by the Sun to other planets tend to be more significant than those of the other planets.

The Sun is associated with vitality and its placement can be an important indicator of physical vitality. The Sun also represents ambition, the urge for power, leadership, creativity, constructiveness, self-reliance, organization and administration, masculinity, individuality, and the ability to carry out heart felt desires. Negative solar traits include arrogance, extravagance, a domineering nature, and a strong desire to control others.

The Sun rules the sign Leo. It is exalted in Aries, is in detriment in Aquarius, and falls in Libra.

☽ The Moon

The Moon is the fastest-moving body in the birth chart, completing an orbit of Earth every 27.32 days. It moves through the entire zodiac in less than one month, moves through an entire sign in a little over two days, and generally gains a degree in under two hours. In comparison, the other major astrological bodies move much more slowly and their positions will change by very small amounts over the course of any given day—or even in the course of a month, in the case of the outer planets.

The word *lunar* is derived from the name of the Greek goddess Luna, who was identified with the Moon. The correlation between the length of the menstrual cycle and the length of a lunar month has influenced cultures all over the world to associate the Moon with women and fertility. Accordingly, lunar deities are almost exclusively female. However, in an exception to this general rule, the Mesopotamian Moon deity was the male divinity Nanna (Sin or Suen), who was the father of the Sun god and was considered to be superior to him.

Astrologically, the Moon is associated with childbirth and represents the principle of creativity in the sense of giving birth to ideas. The Moon's placement in a birth chart can show where and how we nurture as well as seek nurturance, as well as an area of life where we create as well as experience change.

The Moon is responsive and adaptable. Positive Lunar traits include passivity, tenacity, imagination, sensitivity, receptivity, a good memory, and a maternal nature. Negative lunar traits include weak reasoning power, gullibility, narrow-mindedness, unreliability, and lack of commitment. The Moon also represents the subconscious mind, embodying the unconscious patterns of our past.

The Moon rules Cancer, is exalted in Taurus, is in detriment in Capricorn, and falls in Scorpio.

☿ Mercury

Mercury is the nearest planet to the Sun and, because its orbit lies between Earth and the Sun, is always found within twenty-eight degrees of it. It has an orbital period of only eighty-eight days. In the birth chart Mercury appears either in the same sign as the Sun, in the next sign ahead of it, or in the previous sign.

Mercury was named after the Roman god who carried messages between the gods and humanity. Mercury was also associated with the Mesopotamian deity Nabu, the divine scribe who presided over learning, writing, and science.

Like its mythological namesakes, Mercury is associated with writing, teaching, and learning, as well as travel and communication. Mercury represents the conscious aspects of the mind—the faculties of perception, reason, and language that allow us to interact with the world.

The placement of Mercury in a person's chart has a powerful effect on the quality and character of their mind. I have also discovered that it influences the presence or absence of a large number of intellectual gifts or deficits. Positive Mercury traits include good reasoning abilities, perceptivity, versatility, coordination, and communicativeness. Negative Mercury traits include cynicism, biting sarcasm, uncontrolled nervous energy, inconsistency, a hypercritical nature, and lacking a sense of purpose.

Mercury rules Gemini and Virgo, is exalted in Virgo, is in detriment in Sagittarius, and falls in Pisces.

♀ Venus

As seen from the Earth, Venus is never more than forty-eight degrees from the Sun. Venus either occupies the same sign in a birth chart as the Sun, or falls within two signs to either side of it. It has an orbital period of 244 days.

Venus was named after the Roman goddess of fertility and beauty and is associated with love, sociability, and harmony. Although she was the wife of Vulcan, she had love affairs with practically the entire pantheon.

Venus is traditionally thought to represent the center of one's feelings and interpersonal relationships. Its placement in a natal chart shows much about how one relates and what one loves. Venus is considered to be a benefic planet. According to classical astrologers, it has a positive influence second only to Jupiter in potency. Positive Venusian traits include cooperation, harmony, skill in love and the social arts, appreciation of beauty, and a kind and friendly manner. Negative Venusian traits include laziness, indecisiveness, excessive romanticism, a weak will, carelessness, impracticality, and overdependence on others.

Venus rules Taurus and Libra, is exalted in Pisces, is in detriment in Aries, and falls in Virgo.

♂ Mars

Mars is the fourth planet from the Sun. It has an orbital period of 686.98 days.

As a deity, Mars epitomized the warrior. He was also the most despised god in the Pantheon. He continually lost his temper and rushed into battle, often at the wrong time. He was ruled by his passions and his temper was legendary. His two attendants were Phobos (Fear) and Deimos (Panic).

Although in its positive expression Mars represents the motivating force through which one is impelled to act, it is also considered to be a minor malefic, a planet that rules the minor mishaps in one's life. It is second only to Saturn in its negative effect on the birth chart. Mars is associated with aggression, emotional passion, and conflict, as well as spontaneity, impulsiveness, and ambition. Mars represents aggressive energy, defining the active and outgoing traits of a person. Mars shows where one is likely to experience conflict, running to such extremes as violence, bloodshed, knives, guns, murder, or arson. Positive Martian traits include a strong sex drive, defense of the weak, strong leadership, energy, passion, initiative, independence, and enterprise. Negative Martian traits include aggressiveness, selfishness, rudeness, indifference to detail, and boisterousness.

In former times, Mars ruled both Scorpio and Aries. After Pluto was discovered, the rulership of Scorpio was reassigned to it, leaving Mars to rule Aries. Mars is exalted in Capricorn, in detriment in Libra, and falls in Cancer.

♃ Jupiter

Jupiter is the largest planet in the solar system. It has an orbital period of 11.86 years, and stays in each sign of the zodiac for about one year.

In mythology, Jupiter was the ruler of the Roman pantheon of deities, and was associated with storms, victory, and justice. He was known as the protector of the young and the weak. Like his daughter Venus, he showed a great passion for the opposite sex.

Jupiter is called the Greater Benefic and is the most positive planetary influence in the chart, representing the generous, optimistic, and constructive side of the self. Its primary characteristics are expansiveness and good fortune. Jupiter is also related to religion, philosophy, wealth, and success. The area where Jupiter is placed in a birth chart shows a potential for good luck and multiplicity. Positive Jupiter traits include generosity, loyalty, joviality, luck, progressiveness, justice, and opportunism. Negative Jupiter traits include blind optimism, extravagance, conceit, self-indulgence, and unbalanced beliefs.

Jupiter originally ruled both Pisces and Sagittarius, but the modern rulership of Pisces is given to Neptune. Jupiter is exalted in Cancer, in detriment in Gemini, and falls in Capricorn.

♄ Saturn

The farthest planet that can be seen with the unaided eye, Saturn takes 26.46 years to complete an orbit around the Sun. It moves through each sign in about two and a half years.

Saturn, originally the Greek Father of the Gods (Chronos), evolved among the Romans into a god of agriculture. We see the myth again in Italy's Golden Age, with King Saturnus emerging as the founder of civilization and social order.

Saturn has been called the Greater Malefic, traditionally carrying the most negative influence in the birth chart. Once considered the outermost planet in the universe, it came to be associated with limitation. As the slowest-moving planet known to the ancients, it was also attributed to age and wisdom. It is an embodiment of the principle of stability, social order, and the opposite of upheaval. Saturn is also associated with time cycles, the harvest, big business, and with the principle of contraction. It represents the process of bringing what is vague and unformed into manifestation. Positive Saturnian traits include caution, patience, ambition, reliability, thrift, self-discipline, endurance, and responsibility. Negative Saturn associations include selfishness, a dogmatic nature, a life of sorrow and ill health, cruelty, and a tyrannical nature.

Traditionally, Saturn was said to rule both Aquarius and Capricorn. However, after the discovery of Uranus, Saturn was assigned exclusively to Capricorn. Saturn is exalted in Libra, in detriment in Cancer, and falls in Aries.

♅ Uranus

Discovered in 1781 by William Herschel, Uranus is the first of the "modern" planets. Uranus is a giant planet, some 29,300 miles in diameter. It has an unusual axial inclination, tilting more than ninety degrees. Uranus takes 84.01 years to orbit the Sun, staying in each sign of the zodiac for about seven years.

Uranus is the only planet to be named after a Greek rather than a Roman god. This is because the Greek god Chronos, whom the Romans identified with Saturn, was the son of the oldest god, Uranus. With Herschel's discovery, astronomers felt that they had discovered the ancestor of all the planets. This was, of course, not the case.

Uranus was god of the sky. A tyrant who imprisoned his offspring, he was castrated by his son Chronos (Saturn). Some astrologers believe that the more appropriate mythological association for this planet is Prometheus, a trickster and a rebel who stole fire from heaven and gave it to humankind.

Uranus is associated with humanism, ideals, eccentricity, and rebelliousness. It rules sudden, unexpected change, astrology, science, electricity, and occultism. Uranus represents the creative, innovative, freedom-seeking part of the self. Its placement in the chart shows much about how a person expresses his or her creative genius. Positive Uranian traits include kindness, independence, originality, genius, versatility, curiosity, and a strong-willed nature. Negative Uranian traits include eccentricity, perversity, iconoclasm, crankiness, and extreme abnormality.

Uranus rules Aquarius, is exalted in Scorpio, is in detriment in Leo, and falls in Taurus.

♆ Neptune

Neptune orbits between Uranus and Pluto, completing its trip around the Sun every 164.79 years. It stays almost fourteen years in each sign of the zodiac.

Neptune was named after the Roman god of the sea, where he lived in a golden palace. The astrological glyph for Neptune is the trident, which he used to create storms and floods.

Neptune is a mystical and spiritual planet that represents the subtle, intangible side of human existence. It also represents the human imagination and unconscious mind at the individual level (personal unconscious). Positive Neptune traits include idealism, sacrifice, vision, sensitivity, creativity, and inspiration. The negative expressions of this planet are escapism, self-deception, confusion, carelessness, worrying, deceit, and disorganization.

Neptune rules Pisces, is exalted in Cancer, is in detriment in Virgo, and falls in Capricorn.

♀ Pluto

Pluto is the farthest planet from the Sun. It was not discovered until 1930. Pluto completes an orbit of the Sun every 247.69 years, spending anywhere from fifteen to thirty years in each sign.

Pluto was named after the Roman god of the underworld and death. He is remembered in myth as the husband of Persephone, whose yearly visit to the underworld causes the Earth to go barren in winter.

Pluto represents the human collective unconscious, life and death matters, and the will to control and dominate. It also represents basic life drives such as sex, aggression, and the creative and regenerative forces of the body. Pluto is also associated with eruptions, volcanoes, earthquakes, big business, and enforced change. Positive Pluto traits include a flair for big business, financial security, an analytical nature, and regeneration. Negative Pluto traits include an unhealthy unconscious mind, sadism, cruelty, bestiality, and criminal tendencies.

Pluto is said to rule Scorpio, and its exaltation, detriment, and fall have not been conclusively determined.

THE ASPECTS

Planets are in aspect when there are specific angular distances between them in the horoscope chart. These geometric relationships reveal the areas of personality where the native's characteristics can attain full and positive expression, and other areas in which there may be some experience of psychological stress and strain. The major (or *Ptolemaic)* aspects are the *conjunction* (0°), *sextile* (60°), *square* (90°), *trine* (120°), and *opposition* (180°).

Astrologers allow for varying degrees of tolerance, called *orbs*, in identifying these aspects.

The major hard (difficult) aspects come from dividing the horoscope circle into halves and quarters. Squares and oppositions are regarded as hard aspects and usually represent challenges to be faced and overcome. Soft (supportive) aspects come from dividing the circle into thirds and sixths. Sextiles and trines are regarded as soft aspects and usually represent an easy and harmonious combination of forces. The conjunction is indicative of a powerful blending of forces and can be easy or challenging depending on the planets involved.

Minor aspects include the *semisextile* (30°), the *decile* (36°), the *semisquare* (45°), the *quintile* (72°), the *sesquisquare* (135°), the *biquintile* (144°), and—probably the most commonly used of the minor aspects—the *quincunx* or *inconjunct* (150°). Most astrologers, however, confine their interpretations primarily to the major aspects.

THE BIRTH CHART

Around the Earth, the twelve equal signs of the zodiac form an encircling band along the *ecliptic* (the apparent plane of the Sun's orbit, as seen from Earth). Along the ecliptic move the main forces of astrology—the planets. They pass, at differing speeds, out of one of the twelve signs of the zodiac and into the next in a never-ending circuit.

In astrology, the moment of birth is taken as the defining event in the subject's life, and the birth chart—a map of the heavens as seen at the moment and from the place of birth—records the location of the planets within the zodiac at that time and place. The Earth is represented by a small circle in the center of the chart, around which the heavens revolve once every twenty-four hours. (This is a relativistic observation: astrologers are perfectly aware that it is the Earth that is revolving.) Thus, a different sign of the zodiac rises over the horizon every two hours. Accordingly, the birth chart is divided into twelve sections known as *houses*.

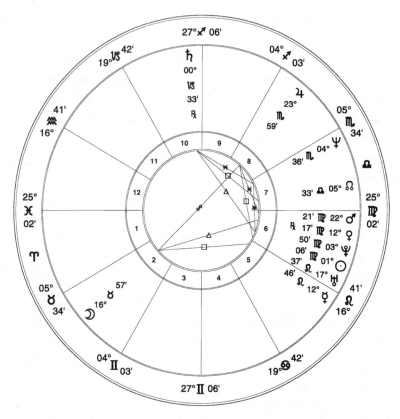

Chart 1: Dr. Mitchell Gibson's Natal Chart (Longitudinal)

Chart 1 shows my birth chart mapped along the traditional circular axis. Based on twelve thirty-degree divisions of the 360-degree zodiac, with its starting point (0° Aries) defined by the Sun's position on the vernal equinox, this circular chart focuses on the longitude of the planets, as well as their position in the twelve houses. This is the format that the vast majority of today's Western astrologers utilize in presenting birth data to clients.

While the longitudinal (circular) chart has been the dominant form used by astrologers for centuries, and has provided us with a great deal of useful data and insight into the inner workings of the human psyche, there is a great deal more information to be gleaned. In addition to traditional longitudinal data, this study makes use of *declinational* data toward this end. In essence, this

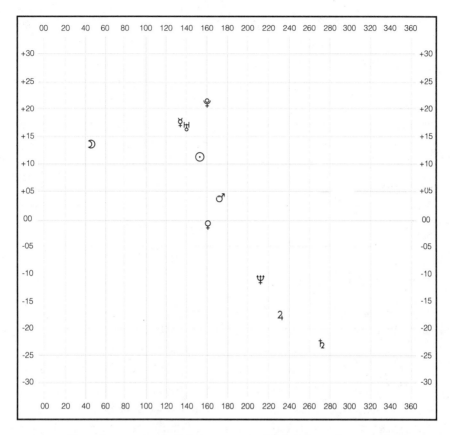

Chart 2: Dr. Mitchell Gibson's Natal Chart (Declinational)

allows the astrologer to plot the position of the planets along an additional axis of reference.

Chart 2 depicts my birth mapped along both the declinational and longitudinal axes. Admittedly, this form is quite different from any other currently in widespread use, but I have discovered that most of the significant planetary relationships that are not at all discernible on the circular (longitudinal) chart are readily seen in the second format. In fact, I have found that there is a vast treasure trove of untapped data within the declinational chart that may change the way we look at birth data altogether. For this reason, I have used this chart form to illustrate the examples in this book. In this format, the longitudinal positions of the planets are shown along the X (horizontal) axis, while their declination (position north or south of the equator) is displayed along the Y (vertical) axis. In the Appendix, I have included a conversion table for those who wish to find the planets' positions in the signs as represented in this form, and a blank declinational chart for you to photocopy and use to plot the planets' positions in this new way.

You will notice there are no house divisions in the declinational chart. For the purposes of this study, I did not use data related to houses or the position of the planets within a particular house, but focused on the planets' positions and aspects. I will expand on the components and construction of this new format in the following chapter.

FATE OR FREE WILL?

The planets, aspects, and other factors in our birth chart are not thought to directly influence us, but to act as guideposts within the unconscious for our actions along the road of life. One of my teachers once told me that one should not look on astrological guidance as a *fait accompli* to unbridled fatalism. Rather, he believed that the chart provides the core blueprint for our choices and exerts a strong influence over our entire destiny, but free will and determined effort provide the remainder of our determining factors. Conversely, a lack of concerted and focused effort could ostensibly increase the unconscious guiding principle contained within the chart.

I have found this to be an invaluable rule of thumb in the interpretation of an individual's chart. I believe that the harder a person works at unfolding the higher possibilities of their lives, the greater the chance that they will overcome the hardships inherent within the karmic boundaries mapped out in the birth chart. I have also found that an intimate knowledge of the latent strengths and weaknesses inherent in the birth chart can and does significantly improve one's chances of realizing their highest destiny. Guidance by a highly trained and experienced astrologer can help one avoid obvious pitfalls and take advantage of the opportunities that present themselves in the course of everyday life.

4 New Advances in Astrology

ASTROLOGY IS ONE OF OUR OLDEST ARTS, AND HAS BEEN RESPONSIBLE for influencing human history more than almost any other single discipline. Computers have allowed birth charts to be created by almost anyone with rudimentary computer skills. However, the actual mechanics of chart preparation and interpretation have remained virtually unchanged.

There are two coordinates on any map used for the location of positions—horizontal (longitude) and vertical (latitude). This same principle applies to the planets and stars in the sky. In astrology, the horizontal coordinates are called longitude and the vertical coordinates are called latitude or declination.

Almost all astrologers use longitudinal coordinates for the birth chart as the sole measure of planetary movement. Longitude refers to the sign or part of the sky in which a particular planet or star resides at any given time—i.e., 22° Leo, 13° Aries, etc. The signs refer to the twelve horizontal sectors that the planets transit during their trek through the sky.

There are, however, equally valid and immensely useful latitudinal (declinational) data for the planets and stars. All of the objects in the sky move vertically as well as horizontally, and this vertical movement has powerful astrological significance. As opposed to astrological guides, astronomical texts always carry both the vertical and horizontal coordinates for the planets and stars.

The declination of all the planets is measured as either north or south of the *celestial equator,* which is the Earth's equator projected into space. Observed from the northern hemisphere, the Sun reaches its maximum height in the sky during the summer solstice, when it is at 23.4° north declination. It reaches its lowest height in the sky during the winter solstice, when it is at 23.4° south declination. This difference in apparent height is caused by the 23.4° axis tilt maintained by the Earth as it revolves around the Sun.

In their excellent book *Astrology Really Works*, the Magi Society presents several new techniques and terms that have been instrumental in expanding the vistas of astrological research. They were the first researchers to use declinations and multiple planet aspects. Their work has been limited to the study of celebrities, financial matters, sports, and a small group of world events. To date, they have not done any definitive work on mental illness or the emotional aspects of human behavior. Therefore, this remains a totally uncharted area, even for those who are involved in the new research.

Astrologers have always maintained that we are influenced by the movements of the planets. It is curious that fully one half of these movements have been virtually ignored by astrologers for 2,000 years. I have found that there is a vast treasure trove of knowledge and untapped data waiting to be mined and analyzed by the evolving research-oriented astrological community. The public at large also deserves to be made privy to the fascinating information hidden in this largely unknown sector of their birth charts.

New Terms

Most of the significant astrological correlations that I have found in the birth charts of clients with mental illnesses have been discovered in the declinations. I will now outline the major terms and definitions that will act as guideposts during our journey into this uncharted territory. Some of these terms were first used by the Magi Society in *Astrology Really Works*. However, many of the terms listed and discussed below are new and are the result of new research findings during the course of my work.

Elevation

Specific aspects and/or declinational positions that affect the basic expression of a planet's energies. Elevations may be positive or negative, depending on the planet's position and/or the planet(s) it interacts with.

Parallel

A declinational planetary interaction in which two celestial bodies are positioned within an orb of two degrees and thirty-four minutes on the same side of the celestial equator.

> Example: Mars +17° 21'
> Jupiter +17 ° 39'

Contraparallel

A declinational planetary interaction in which two celestial bodies are positioned within an orb of two degrees and thirty-four minutes on opposite sides of the celestial equator.

> Example: Mars +17° 21'
> Jupiter -17° 39'

Planetary Eclipse

An event that occurs when two planets are simultaneously in conjunction and parallel to each other. Planetary eclipses are fairly common occurrences.

Binary Eclipse

An event that occurs when three planets are simultaneously in conjunction and parallel to each other. Binary planetary eclipses are very uncommon occurrences

Plenary Eclipse

An event that occurs when four or more planets are simultaneously in conjunction and parallel to each other. Plenary eclipses are exceptionally rare occurrences.

Triangle Elevation

A declinational planetary interaction wherein three celestial bodies are parallel or contraparallel to each other (or any combination thereof) at the same time. All planets within a triangle elevation must be either parallel or contraparallel to all other planets within the triangle. Triangle elevations are fairly common.

Example: Mars +17° 21'
Jupiter +17° 39'
Uranus -18° 02'

Quad Elevation

A declinational planetary interaction wherein four celestial bodies are parallel or contraparallel to each other (or any combination thereof) at the same time. All planets in a quad elevation must be parallel or contraparallel to all other planets within the quad. Quad elevations are uncommon.

Example: Mars +17° 21'
Jupiter +17° 39'
Uranus -18° 02'
Neptune +18° 12'

Plenary Elevation

A declinational planetary interaction wherein five celestial bodies are parallel or contraparallel to each other (or any combination thereof) at the same time. All planets within a plenary elevation must be parallel or contraparallel to all other planets within the elevation. Plenary elevations are rare.

Example: Mars +17° 02'
Jupiter +17° 39'
Uranus -18° 02'
Neptune -18° 20'
Venus +17° 10'

Band Elevation

A declinational planetary interaction wherein six celestial bodies are parallel or contraparallel to each other (or any combination thereof) at the same time. All planets within a band elevation must be parallel or contraparallel to all other planets within the elevation. Band elevations are extremely rare.

Example: Mars +17° 02'
Jupiter +18° 02'
Uranus -18° 21'
Neptune -18° 10'
Mercury +17° 30'
Venus +17° 10'

Elevation by High Declination

The declinational position of a celestial body when it is found between 21° and 23° 30' on either side of the celestial equator. Often referred to in its abbreviated form **Hidek.**

Example: Jupiter +22° 12'

Elevation by Extreme Declination

The declinational position of a celestial body when it is found above 23° 30' on either side of the celestial equator. Often referred to in its abbreviated form **Exdek.**

Example: Moon -25° 16'

Elevation by Proximity

The declinational position of two celestial bodies when they are found within 30' of each other in a parallel or contraparallel relationship. Proximity elevations are uncommon.

Example: Jupiter +17° 21'
Venus -17° 10'

Degree of Elevation

The number of elevations (positive or negative) that a particular planet may have in a chart. When Mercury has a fourth-degree negative in a chart it means that within that particular chart, Mercury has four negative elevations. The greater the number of elevations (positive or negative) that a planet has within a chart, the greater its influence on the native.

Grand Elevation

A special condition when a planet has six or more elevations within a chart. The six elevations must be either positive or negative. (The sum of the positive and negative elevations of a planet within a chart does not indicate the presence of a grand elevation.) For example, if Venus has eight positive elevations within a chart, that particular chart is said to have a grand elevation of Venus.

The presence of a grand elevation of a planet within a chart indicates an area of great influence and activity. Most charts have one to three grand elevations, though it is not uncommon for a chart to possess seven or eight grand elevations. A grand elevation is considered to be "high order when a planet displays nine or more positive or negative elevations."

Multiple grand elevations indicate a greater than normal amount of longitudinal and declinational interactivity among the planets within a chart. This enhanced number of planetary interactions can result in greater positive or negative stress on the native depending on the type of elevations involved.

General Planetary Index (GPI)

The sum of all the positive and negative elevations within a chart. A high number means that a chart has a high degree of interactivity among the planets. The general planetary index of a group of charts may be calculated by averaging the individual general planetary activity indices of each chart within the group.

Positive/Negative Ratio (P/N)

A fraction that equals the total number of positive elevations within a chart or group of charts divided by the total number of negative elevations. A high P/N ratio denotes a high number of positive elevations relative to the number of negative elevations. The P/N ratio is a relative measure of the amount of constructive versus destructive energy latent within a chart and may be a positive or negative number.

Planetary Index

The sum of the positive and negative elevations of a particular planet multiplied by 100. It may be positive or negative and is used as a measure of the relative activity of a planet in a chart.

Temporal Environment Index

A number arrived at by multiplying the GPI of a chart by the P/N times 100. The temporal environment index refers to the positive or negative energy surrounding the time of the casting of a chart or the start of a particular event. A positive temporal environment is very helpful for the completion of constructive events and for fostering harmonious actions. A negative temporal environment is useful for destructive purposes and it is not recommended for the initiation of constructive activities. Activities started within a positive temporal environment tend to last longer and remain more harmonious than similar events that are initiated within a negative temporal environment. Individuals born within a negative temporal environment tend to have a greater amount of disharmony and chaos within their lives than people born in a positive temporal environment. The temporal environment index is calculated as follows:

Example: $34.69 \times 0.833 \times 100 = 2889.677$.

Cardinal Elevation

A planetary elevation that occurs as a marker aspect for more than one mental illness.

Karmic Index

A number that refers to a relative measure of the positive and negative growth potential within a birth chart.

The positive karmic index is calculated as follows: (Sun index + Jupiter index + Venus index) x P/N.

The negative karmic index is calculated as follows: (Saturn index + Mars index) divided by P/N.

Complexity Index

The sum of the triangles, quads, eclipses, plenary, band, and proximity elevations within a chart.

The terms listed above form the core of a new paradigm in astrology. The following chapters will focus on how these new concepts may be utilized to examine the birth chart in an all-new system—one designed to provide tools with which the modern astrologer may more deeply explore the mysteries of the sky.

CALCULATING A MODERN ASTROLOGY CHART

I am in the process of designing software that will automatically erect and calculate all of the measurements outlined below. However, I realize that there will be those who will not wish to wait for that particular innovation, so I am providing the following information that the intelligent layperson as well as the trained astrologer may follow in order to erect a modern astrology chart.

Longitudinal Measurements

1. Assemble the information necessary to run a modern astrology chart: the birth date, place of birth, and time of birth (if available). Unless you can erect charts by hand and have an ephemeris that also lists planetary declinations, you will need astrological software that calculates declinational as well as longitudinal planetary coordinates. (Most current professional-level programs do this automatically.)

2. After generating a complete list of conjunctions, trines, sextiles, squares, oppositions, you will need to assign a positive or negative value to each aspect, as follows:

   All squares and oppositions are negative.

   All conjunctions, trines, and sextiles are positive when they do not involve Saturn.

   Any aspects involving Saturn are negative.

   Any aspects involving any combination of Mars, Sun, Jupiter, and Venus are positive.

   All other aspects involving Mars are negative.

   Longitudinal proximity elevations are calculated by determining which planets are within a ten-degree radius of each other on the longitudinal chart.

   All longitudinal proximity elevations involving Saturn and/or Mars are negative except those involving the Sun, Jupiter, and Venus. All longitudinal proximity elevations not involving Saturn are positive.

3. The total number of aspects within the longitudes are then calculated by adding together all of the conjunctions, trines, sextiles, squares, oppositions, and longitudinal proximity elevations. The positive elevations and the negative elevations are tallied into separate groups.

Declinational Measurements

4. Parallels and contraparallels are identified using the declinational coordinates of the natal chart. I have adopted the orb of two degrees, thirty four minutes as the orb of reference for parallels and contraparallels.

   All parallels and contraparallels that involve Saturn are negative.

   If a planet is parallel or contraparallel to another planet that is contraparallel or parallel to Saturn, all declinational aspects involving that planet are also negative. This is true even if the planet(s) involved are the Sun, Jupiter, and Venus.

All parallels and contraparallels involving Mars are negative, except those involving the Sun, Jupiter, and Venus.

If a planet is parallel or contraparallel to the Sun, Jupiter, or Venus, any parallel or contraparallel it creates with Mars is considered to be positive.

5. Identify the Triangle elevations (three planets forming a parallel or contraparallel relationship to all other planets within the Triangle.

A Triangle is considered to be negative if it involves Saturn as one of the three planets.

A Triangle is considered to be negative if it involves Mars as one of the three planets, except when at least one of the three planets involved is the Sun, Jupiter, or Venus.

If a planet is involved in a positive Triangle, it is credited with an additional positive elevation for each positive Triangle it is part of.

If a planet is involved in a negative Triangle, it is credited with an additional negative elevation for each negative Triangle it is part of.

6. Identify the Quad elevations (four planets that form a parallel or contraparallel relationship with each of the others).

If the Quad involves Saturn, it is given a negative value.

If the Quad involves Mars it is given a negative value, However, if the Sun, Jupiter, and/or Venus are also involved, then the Quad is considered to have a positive value.

If a planet is involved in a positive Quad, then it is credited with an additional positive elevation for each positive Quad that it is involved in.

If a planet is involved in a negative Quad, then it is credited with an additional negative elevation for each negative Quad that it is part of.

7. Identify the Plenary elevations (five planets forming a parallel or contraparallel relationship with each of the others).

   All Plenary elevations involving Saturn are negative.

   All Plenary elevations involving Mars are negative, except those that also involve the Sun, Jupiter, and/or Venus.

   The value of Plenary elevations is calculated in the same manner as that of Triangles and Quads.

8. Identify the Band elevations (six planets forming a parallel or contraparallel with each of the others).

   All band elevations involving Saturn are negative.

   All band elevations involving Mars are negative except those that involve the Sun, Jupiter,or Venus.

   The value of band elevations is calculated in the same manner as Triangles, Quads, and plenaries.

9. Identify the Hidek elevations (whenever a planet is found in a declinational position between 21° and 23° 30' on either side of the celestial equator).

   If a planet in the Hidek position is parallel or contraparallel to Saturn, the elevation is negative.

   If a Hidek planet is parallel or contraparallel to a planet that is parallel or contraparallel to Saturn, its value in that elevation is negative.

   If the Sun, Jupiter, or Venus are parallel or contraparallel to a Hidek planet but are not themselves parallel or contraparallel to Saturn, the value of the planet in the Hidek elevation is positive.

   If a Hidek planet is parallel or contraparallel to Mars, the value of planet is negative in that elevation.

If the Sun, Jupiter, or Venus is parallel or contra-parallel to a Hidek planet that is parallel or contra-parallel to Mars, the elevation is positive.

10. Identify the Exdek elevations (when a planet is found above 23° 30' on either side of the celestial equator).

All Exdek planets are negative unless they are parallel or contraparallel to the Sun, Jupiter, or Venus. In that case, the Sun, Jupiter, or Venus must not form a parallel or contraparallel aspect to Saturn, and they must not be in the Exdek position themselves.

11. Identify the Proximity elevations (when two planets are found within thirty minutes of declination to each other within a particular elevation). The value of the elevation is not changed by any additional proximity enhancement.

12. The total number of elevations within the declinations (positive and negative) is tallied to be used as a part of the calculation of the GPI.

Bilevel Elevations

13. Identify all planetary eclipses, which occur when two planets are parallel and in conjunction to each other. Planetary eclipses are not assigned separate positive or negative values and are interpreted on an individual basis.

A binary eclipse occurs when three planets are parallel and in conjunction to each other at the same time.

A Plenary eclipse occurs when four or more planets are parallel and in conjunction to each other at the same time.

14. Degrees of elevation are calculated by adding the total number of elevations for each planet. A planet with one elevation is has a first-degree elevation, a planet with two elevations has a second-degree elevation, etc. A

planet with six or more elevations is said to have a grand elevation.

15. Planetary indices are calculated by adding the total number of elevations for each planet (irrespective of positive and negative values) and multiplying by 100. For example, if the Sun has a positive index of 5 and a negative of 2, its planetary index is +300.(Note: Planetary eclipses are not used in the calculation of planetary indices.)

Summary Indices

16. The GPI is found by adding the total of all the longitudinal and declinational elevations within a chart. (Note: Planetary eclipses are not used in the calculation of the GPI or P/N.)

17. The P/N is calculated by dividing the positive elevations by the total number of negative elevations.

18. The temporal index is calculated by multiplying the GPI by the P/N (100).

19. The positive karmic index is calculated as follows: (Sun index + Jupiter index + Venus index) x P/N.

20. The negative karmic index is calculated as follows: (Saturn index + Mars index) / P/N.

21. The complexity index is derived by adding the total number of Triangles, Quads, eclipses, Plenaries, bands,and proximity elevations.

A SAMPLE WORKSHEET

In order to clarify the steps given above, I will now present an example, using my own natal chart as the basis. First, the birth information must be gathered and the natal chart must be calculated. (The resulting data is presented below.) Afterward, the longitudinal, declinational, and bilevel elevations will be noted, then the individual planetary indices, followed by the summary indices.

Chart Data: Mitchell E. Gibson, M.D.			
08-24-59 / 7:55 P.M. EST / 079W28 / 35N12			
Planet	Longitude	℞	Declination
☉	01° ♍ 06'		11°N05'
☽	16° ♉ 57'		13°N30'
☿	12° ♌ 46'		16°N41'
♀	12° ♍ 17'	℞	00°S 23'
♂	22° ♍ 21'		03°N48'
♃	23° ♏ 59'		18°S 03'
♄	00° ♑ 33'	℞	22°S38'
♅	17° ♌ 37'		16°N11'
♆	04° ♏ 36'		11°S25'
♇	03° ♍ 50'		21°N02'

Longitudinal Elevations

Conjunctions: ☉-♇, ☿-♅

Trines: ☉-♄, ☽-♀, ♄-♇, ☽-♇, ☽-♂

Sextiles: ☉-♆, ♂-♃, ♄-♆, ♆-♇

Squares: ☉-♃, ☽-☿, ☽-♅, ♃-♅

Oppositions: ☽-♃

Longitudinal proximity (within ten degrees): ♀-♂, ♀-♇

Positive longitudinal elevations: 9

Negative longitudinal elevations: 9

Declinational Elevations

Parallels: ☉-☽, ☿-♅

Contraparallels: ☉-♆, ☽-♆, ☿-♃, ♄-♇, ♃-♅

Triangle elevations: ☉-☽-♆, ☿-♃-♅

Quad elevations: None

Plenary elevations: None

Band elevations: None

Declinational Elevations

High declination (Hidek): ♄ , ♀

Extreme declination (Exdek): None

Proximity elevations: ☿ -♅ parallel, ☉-♆ contraparallel

Positive declinational elevations: 10

Negative declinational elevations: 3

Bilevel elevations (combined declination and longitude)

Planetary eclipses (two planets): ☿ -♅

Binary eclipses (three planets): None

Plenary eclipses (four or more planets): None

First degree elevations: ☿ , ♂ (negative)

Second degree elevations: ♂ (positive); ☉, ♅, ♆ (negative)

Third degree elevations: ♀ (positive); ♃ , ♀ (negative)

Fourth degree elevations: ♃ ,♀ (positive)

Fifth degree elevations: ☽, ☿ , ♅ (positive); ☽, ♄ (negative)

Grand elevations: ☉ +6, ♆ +6

Planetary indices

Sun index: +400

Moon index: 000

Mercury index: +400

Venus index: +300

Mars index: +100

Jupiter index: +100

Saturn index: -500

Uranus index: +300

Neptune index: +400

Pluto index: +100

Summary Indices

GPI: 31

P/N: +1.5833

Temporal Index: +4,924

Positive Karmic Index: (400+100+300) x 1.5833 = 1,267

Negative Karmic Index: (500+100) / 1.5833 = 379

Complexity Index: 5

5   The Control Group

THE CONTROL GROUP IS AN INTEGRAL PART OF ANY MEANINGFUL study designed to probe the mysteries of science. The main purpose it serves is to provide a baseline of data by which the experimental data in question may be measured and compared. In this way, new information is generated that delineates what would have transpired without test variables and those phenomena that are truly influenced by the test variables.

For example, if one wanted to identify the efficacy of a new medication, one would give the medication to two groups of patients. One group would receive the test medication (the test group), and another group would receive a placebo (the control group). At the end of the study, both groups would be compared for the presence or absence of the desired effect. However, the control group would represent the part of the study that would identify how well the new medication truly works when compared to giving the patient a "sugar pill." Surprisingly, the "placebo effect" is not equivalent to giving no treatment, as many well-controlled scientific studies have shown. This fact of science remains largely unexplained. Nevertheless, this technique provides scientists with a tool that has yielded countless benefits in research.

In this study, five groups were included in the research protocol and one group functioned as the control group. The five test groups were patients who had been given DSM-IV diagnoses of the most common mental illnesses known: major depression, schizophrenia, attention deficit hyperactivity disorder (ADHD), anxiety disorders, and addictive disorders. The control group consisted of twenty-four people who had no history of mental illness and had never received psychiatric treatment. The control group was comprised of comparable age range and gender ratios as the test groups.

Five variables were measured in the control group as a method of establishing a baseline of data indices by which to compare the test patients. These variables were:

- General planetary index (GPI)
- Positive/Negative ratio (P/N)
- Planetary indices
- Grand elevations
- Number of specific planetary markers for mental illness

The average of the twenty-four individual GPIs in the control group was taken as the overall GPI for the control group, revealing an activity level of 27.96 elevations (rounded to twenty-eight).This figure was used as a baseline measure for all succeeding test groups.

The overall P/N was also calculated as the average of the twenty-four individual P/Ns, resulting in a figure of +1.16 for the control group. This indicates a greater number of positive elevations per chart than negative elevations. As we will see, this fact has great relevance when we examine the test groups.

The planetary indices for each individual planet in the control group were added next, resulting in these sums:

Sun: +181

Moon: +112

Mercury: +170

Venus: +133

Mars: -450

Jupiter +194

Saturn: -604

Uranus: +137

Neptune: +148

Pluto: +112

All elevations involving Saturn are considered to be negative. All elevations involving Mars are considered to be negative, except those where the Sun, Jupiter, or Venus are involved, in which case they are positive. This causes the indices involving Saturn and Mars to be more negative than that of the other planets.

Next, grand elevations were calculated for each control chart. Grand elevations reveal areas within a chart where extremely strong forces are focused. A planet was considered to have a grand elevation if it had at least six positive or negative elevations in a chart. Since the average chart held a Saturn grand elevation, it was not considered as one of the marker aspects for the control or test groups.

The average number of grand elevations per chart in the control group was 2.8. The most common grand elevations in the control group were Sun (10), Jupiter (8), and Pluto (8).

Each chart was then analyzed for the presence of individual marker aspects for each mental illness. The average number of identified marker aspects for each mental illness was calculated for the control group, with the following results:

Major depression: 2.95 (rounded to 3)

Anxiety disorder: 1.5 (rounded to 2)

Schizophrenia: 3.29 (rounded to 3)

ADHD: 2.79 (rounded to 3)

Addictive disease: 2.33 (rounded to 2)

The control charts were found to have a significantly lower average number of marker aspects ("signs") than the test groups. The average number of marker aspects for the test groups is listed below:

Major depression: 9.83 (rounded to 10)

Anxiety disorder: 5.10 (rounded to 5)

Schizophrenia: 6.86 (rounded to 7)

ADHD: 13.31 (rounded to 13)

Addictive disease: 7.54 (rounded to 8)

In graph form, the contrasts become easily apparent. Clearly, the test group's marker aspects for mental illness are significantly higher than can be accounted for by chance.

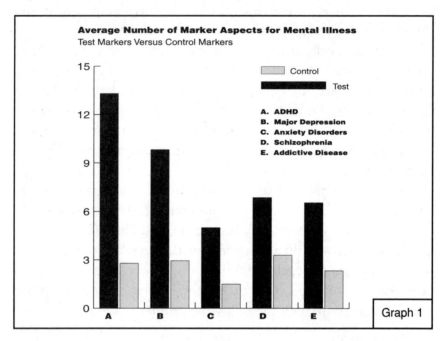

Average Number of Marker Aspects for Mental Illness
Test Markers Versus Control Markers

Control
Test

A. ADHD
B. Major Depression
C. Anxiety Disorders
D. Schizophrenia
E. Addictive Disease

Graph 1

The following five charts are examples selected from the control group. All charts are identified by number in order to protect the identity of the individuals within each of the groups.

CHART 3: CONTROL 13

Major depression: **1**
    (Mercury conjunct Venus)

Anxiety disorder: **0**

Schizophrenia: **1**
    (Mercury conjunct Venus)

ADHD: **1**
    (Saturn parallel Uranus)

Addictive disease: **0**

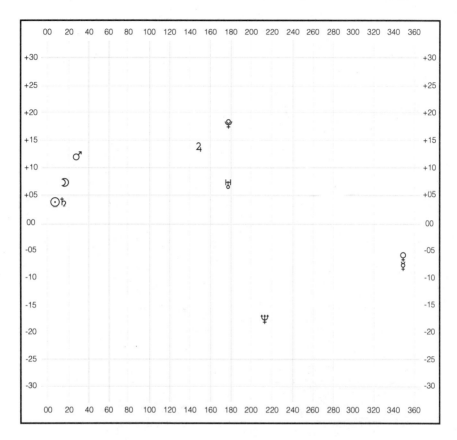

Chart 3: Control 13

The GPI is 22 and the P/N is 1.44. This individual has no history of mental illness.

CHART 4: CONTROL 4

This chart contains a slightly above-average number of markers for major depression, but it is still well below the overall averages for the test group.

Major depression: **4**
   (Uranus square Neptune / Pluto parallel Uranus / Venus parallel Moon / Hidek Pluto)

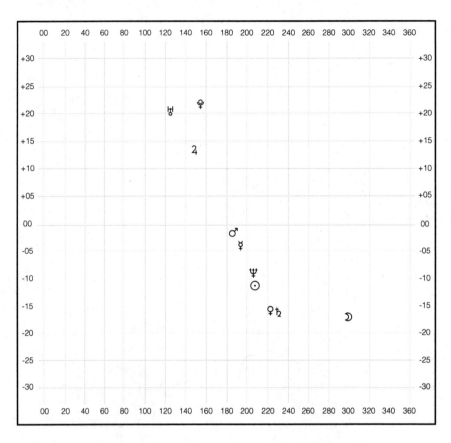

Chart 4: Control 4

Anxiety disorders: 0

Schizophrenia: 3
 (Uranus square Neptune / Hidek Pluto / Grand Elevation
 of the Moon. [Moon conjunct Mars, Moon square Neptune, Moon square Sun, Venus parallel Moon, Saturn-
 Venus-Moon triangle, Moon-Uranus opposition.])

ADHD: 1
 (Uranus square Neptune)

Addictive disease: 0

The GPI is 25 and the P/N is -0.66. This individual has no history of mental illness.

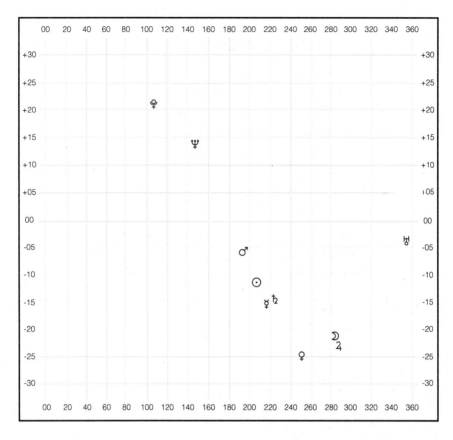

Chart 5: Control 27

CHART 5: CONTROL 27

Major depression: **2**
   (Sun sextile Neptune / Exdek Venus)

Anxiety disorder: **2**
   (Saturn parallel Mercury / Sun contraparallel Neptune)

Schizophrenia: **1**
   (Grand Elevation of the Moon [Jupiter conjunct Moon,
   Jupiter parallel Moon, Pluto contraparallel Moon, Pluto
   contraparallel Moon, Jupiter-Pluto-Moon triangle,
   Hidek Moon])

ADHD **2**
   (Sun sextile Neptune / Sun contraparallel Neptune)

Addictive disease: **3**
   (Saturn trine Pluto / Saturn parallel Mercury / Jupiter-Moon eclipse)

The GPI is 28 and the P/N is +1.15.

CHART 6: CONTROL 24

Major depression: **0**

Anxiety disorders: **0**

Schizophrenia: **2**
   (Saturn trine Moon / Neptune parallel Moon)

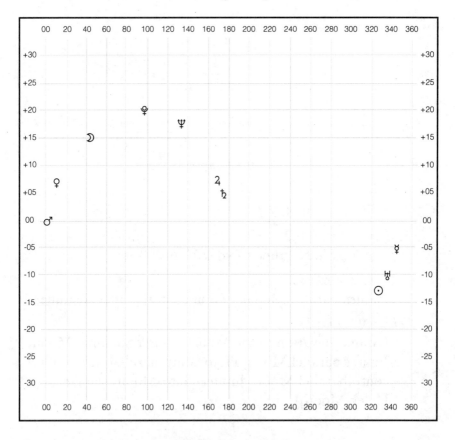

Chart 6: Control 24

ADHD 1
(Pluto square Venus)

Addictive disease: 0

The GPI is 20 and the P/N is -0.66.

CHART 7: CONTROL 2

This individual has a very active chart, with a GPI of 50 (the average is 28). Note that despite this high level of activity, this chart possesses only one group of marker aspects for mental illness that equals the average for the test group. To date, this person has no history of mental illness, but may be astrologically predisposed to the development of schizophrenia or depression.

Major depression: **6**
(Sun conjunct Mercury / Mercury conjunct Venus / Exdek Moon / Jupiter contraparallel Mercury / Grand Elevation of the Sun [Sun conjunct Neptune, conjunct Mercury, sextile Mars, sextile Pluto, sextile Uranus, parallel Pluto, parallel Neptune, parallel Jupiter] / Plenary Elevation involving Sun-Jupiter-Pluto-Neptune-Venus / Proximity Elevation: Sun parallel Venus] / Grand Elevation of Pluto [Pluto conjunct Uranus, trine Moon, sextile Sun, sextile Venus, sextile Mercury, sextile Neptune, parallel Sun, parallel Venus, parallel Neptune, plenary elevation of Pluto involving Sun-Jupiter-Pluto-Neptune-Venus])

Anxiety disorder: **3**
(Grand Elevations of Sun* and Venus [Venus conjunct Neptune, conjunct Mercury, sextile Mars, sextile Pluto, sextile Uranus, contraparallel Pluto, parallel Neptune, parallel Jupiter] / Plenary Elevation involving Sun-Jupiter-Pluto-Neptune-Venus / Proximity Elevation: Sun parallel Venus)

Schizophrenia: **7**
(Grand Elevations of Sun** and Mercury [Mercury conjunct Venus, conjunct Sun, conjunct Neptune, sextile

---

* See above
** See above

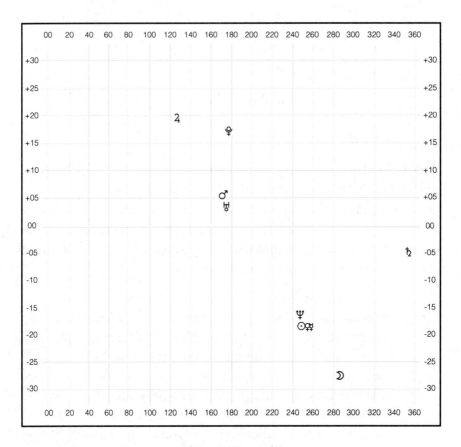

Chart 7: Control 2

Pluto, sextile Uranus] / Proximity elevation: Mercury
contraparallel Jupiter/ Mercury conjunct Venus / Mars
sextile Venus / Sun-Mercury parallel)

ADHD: **4**

(Uranus sextile Mercury / Mercury sextile Mars / Sun
parallel Venus / Grand Elevation of Neptune [Sun conjunct Neptune, Neptune conjunct Venus, Uranus sextile
Neptune, Pluto sextile Neptune, Pluto parallel Neptune,
Sun parallel Neptune, Plenary Elevation of Neptune
involving Sun-Jupiter-Pluto-Neptune-Venus, Neptune
conjunct Mercury])

Addictive disease: **3**

> (Grand Elevation of Pluto [Pluto conjunct Uranus, trine
> Moon, sextile Sun, sextile Venus, sextile Mercury, sextile
> Neptune, parallel Sun, parallel Venus, parallel Neptune,
> · plenary elevation of Pluto involving Sun-Jupiter-Pluto-
> Neptune-Venus])

Of all the mental illnesses, this person would be most susceptible to major depression. Nevertheless, the overall GPI is 50 and
the P/N is +1.50: a hopeful sign.

SUMMARY

The data for the control group indicate that the most active planets with positive elevations were Jupiter and the Sun. The most
active planets with negative values for the elevations were Mars
and Saturn. Granted, Saturn and Mars are weighted toward the
negative in this system, but it is still significant to note that all of
the other planetary indices were in the positive range. The data
relating to the Sun and Jupiter are very much in keeping with
traditional lore that states that they are the most benefic bodies
in the sky.

The P/N of the control group would seem to indicate that, on
the average, people with no history of mental illness tend to have
a rough balance of positive and negative planetary elevations. The
most common grand elevations within the control group were of
the Sun and Jupiter. This again is in keeping with ancient folklore
that states that these two bodies are great benefics. On the average, the control charts possessed a low number of marker aspects
for mental illness when compared to the test group. Most of the
control charts did, however, have some of the marker aspects for
many of the illnesses studied. While the presence of the marker
aspects does not guarantee the development of a mental illness, it
may indicate an astrological predisposition toward that particular
illness. As we examine the test charts, we can more carefully inves-
tigate this hypothesis.

6 Major Depression

WITH AN EXTENSIVE HISTORY IN WESTERN SOCIETY SINCE HIPPOCRATES first described it as a medical illness, major depression is one of the most common mental illnesses in the world today. There are an estimated 17.6 million adult Americans suffering from depression, and only 6 million are receiving treatment. The 11.6 million under-treated represent a major health risk, a 15% likelihood of suicide, an estimated annual price tag of $43 billion in direct and indirect costs, and an enormous challenge for health professionals.

The onset of depression generally occurs when a person is in their twenties or thirties (although there is an early-onset type that begins before age twenty-one), but it can occur at any time. Major depression is expected to affect 10% of men and 20% of women at some point in their lives. However, chronic recurrent depression is significantly rarer and does not affect as large a segment of the population.

The theories regarding the causes of major depression are numerous. It is generally thought to be associated with a hyper-active hypothalamic-pituitary-adrenal axis which leads to increased cortisol secretion. Most of the drugs that are designed to treat depression are focused on correcting imbalances within the serotonin-norepinephrine hormonal systems. Prozac®, an antidepressant, is easily one of the most well-known and most prescribed drugs in the world. It works by inhibiting the absorption of serotonin into the body.

Some clinicians believe depression is caused by a negative self-image or a negative interpretation of experience. Psychoanalytic theory states that depression is associated with a pathologic form of mourning caused by a perceived loss.

Recent research involving the Borna disease virus, once thought to infect farm and domestic animals only, points to a link with some cases of human depression. Dr. Liv Bode described the first two patients with severe depression and evidence of Borna disease virus (BDV) infection, whose depressive symptoms were resolved several weeks after treatment with the antiviral agent amantadine sulfate. Dr. Bode of the prestigious Robert Koch-Institut, Berlin, and her associates are now starting a placebo-controlled trial to test the antidepressant effects of this antiviral therapy in patients with major depression.

The Diagnostic and Statistical Manual IV (DSM-IV) is the gold standard by which all psychiatric clinical diagnoses are measured. The DSM-IV criteria for major depression are:

- Depressed mood (can be irritable mood in children and adolescents) most of the day, nearly every day, as indicated either by subjective account or observation by others
- Markedly diminished interest or pleasure in all, or almost all, activities most of the day, nearly every day (as indicated either by subjective account or observation by others of apathy most of the time)
- Significant weight loss or weight gain when not dieting (e.g., more than 5% body weight in a month), or decrease or increase in appetite nearly every day
- Insomnia or hypersomnia nearly every day
- Psychomotor agitation or retardation nearly every day (observable by others, not merely subjective feelings of restlessness or being slowed down)
- Fatigue or loss of energy nearly every day
- Feelings of worthlessness or excessive or inappropriate guilt (which may be delusional) nearly every day (not merely self-reproach or guilt about being sick)

- Diminished ability to think or concentrate, or indecisiveness, nearly every day (either by subjective account or as observed by others)
- Recurrent thoughts of death (not just fear of dying), recurrent suicidal ideation without a specific plan, or a suicide attempt or a specific plan for committing suicide*

STUDY 1: MAJOR DEPRESSION

All of the causes of depression are not yet known and there may be numerous undiscovered contributing factors. This study is designed to elucidate another possible cause of depression.

I studied the birth charts of eighteen patients with a DSM-IV diagnosis of major depression. Each of the patients actively exhibited at least five of the above symptoms for at least two weeks. All had been treated for depression for at least two years, and most have been hospitalized at least once for the disorder.

Below are the data for this eighteen-person test group, contrasted with that of the control group. As seen here and in Graph 2 (see page 58), there are significant differences in the planetary activity of the two groups.

Planetary Indices	Test Group	Control Group	(Change)
Sun	+225	+181	+19.6%
Moon	+128	+112	+12.5%
Mercury	+138	+170	-18.8%
Venus	+214	+133	+62.1%
Mars	-426	-450	-5.3%
Jupiter	+179	+194	-7.7%
Saturn	-494	-604	-18.2%
Uranus	+152	+137	+9.9%
Neptune	+231	+148	+64.1%
Pluto	+145	+112	+22.8%

* Reprinted with permission from the Diagnostic and Statistical Manual of Mental Disorders, Fourth Edition. Copyright 1994 American Psychiatric Association.

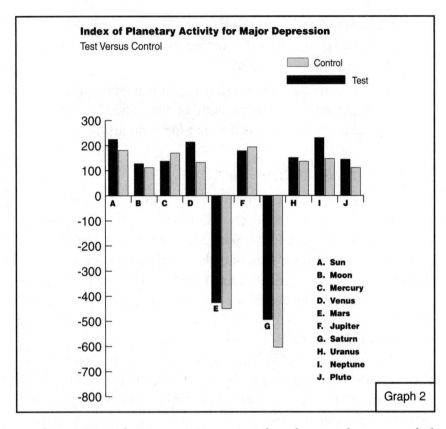

Graph 2

Looking at Graph 3 (page 59), we see that the test charts revealed a greater than threefold increase in the average number of marker aspects for major depression when compared to the control charts.

Markers for Major Depression (43)

Conjunctions:
> Sun/Pluto, Sun/Mercury, Pluto/Mercury, Mercury/Venus, Venus/Uranus

Trines:
> Venus/Jupiter, Jupiter/Pluto, Uranus/Neptune

Sextiles:
> Saturn/Uranus, Sun/Neptune, Moon/Uranus, Venus/Neptune, Moon/Pluto

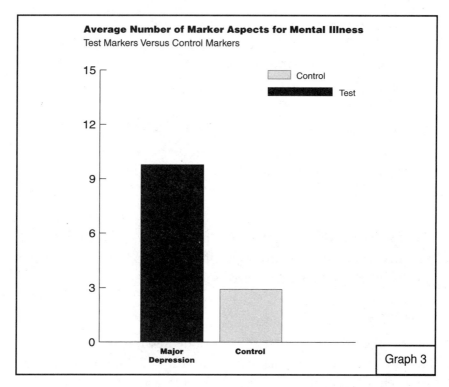

Average Number of Marker Aspects for Mental Illness
Test Markers Versus Control Markers

Graph 3

Squares:
   Saturn/Neptune, Uranus/Neptune, Moon/Mercury
Parallels:
   Saturn/Pluto, Sun/Mercury, Pluto/Mars, Venus/Moon,
   Uranus/Moon, Pluto/Uranus
Contraparallels:
   Jupiter/Neptune, Jupiter/Mercury, Saturn/Pluto,
   Jupiter/Uranus, Saturn/Mercury, Pluto/Mercury
Triangles:
   Saturn-Pluto-Mars, Mars-Moon-Uranus
Hidek:
   Pluto, Uranus, Saturn
Exdek:
   Mars, Moon, Venus

Proximity elevations:
    Pluto/Mars parallel, Pluto/Mercury contraparallel,
    Saturn/Pluto parallel

Eclipse:
    Sun-Mercury

Grand Elevations:
    Mars, Sun, Pluto

The GPI of the test group is 27.89, and the P/N is +1.13.

The following six examples present the histories and charts of patients who display many signs of major depression. All names used to identify the patients are pseudonyms.

HENRY

Henry experienced his first episode of depression at the age of ten. His mother noticed that he was isolative and did not play with the other children in the same way his brothers and sisters did. His grades were below average and his teachers noticed that he cried easily and often got into fights with his peers. When he was twelve years old, Henry took an overdose of aspirin in a suicide attempt. He was hospitalized at that time for five weeks.

For the next ten years he experienced recurrent episodes of depression that interfered with his ability to function. He tried five different antidepressants which all worked to varying degrees, but had to stop them because of problematic side effects. When he was thirty-one, he received ECT (electro-convulsive therapy) and for the first time in his life he began to feel that he could begin to live normally. Prior to that treatment, he had attempted suicide twelve times and had been hospitalized a total of eighteen times for the treatment of depression. He currently continues to receive individual psychotherapy and antidepressant medication, but remains incapable of self-support.

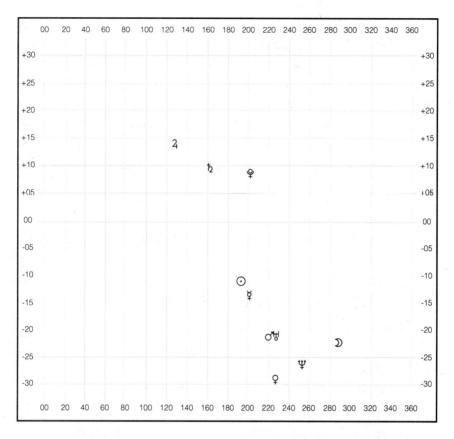

Chart 8: Henry

Henry has a number of problematic marker aspects in his birth chart. Most notable are a Grand Elevation of Mars, the Saturn/Pluto parallel, and the proximity elevation of his Pluto/Mercury contraparallel—all very distinct and prominent markers for depression. His Mars Grand Elevation consists of six negative elevations and casts a focus of negative Mars energy into his birth chart. The Saturn/Pluto parallel is one of the most difficult patterns I have encountered in association with mental illness. It is one of the strongest associations for chronic recurrent unipolar depression that I have encountered—even stronger since the parallel is also elevated by proximity.

The Saturn/Pluto contraparallel is a little less problematic but is still associated with recurrent unipolar depression. The Pluto/Mercury contraparallel is a cardinal sign of mental illness and is a marker aspect for major depression and schizophrenia. The Pluto/Mercury contraparallel in Henry's chart is also elevated by proximity, a fact which adds exceedingly to its power and influence. Henry has three other cardinal signs of mental illness: Jupiter/Neptune contraparallel, Saturn/Pluto parallel, and Sun/Neptune sextile.

Markers for Major Depression (18)

Conjunctions:
> Sun/Pluto, Mercury/Pluto, Sun/Mercury, Venus/Uranus

Sextiles:
> Sun/Neptune, Saturn/Uranus

Squares:
> Moon/Mercury, Saturn/Neptune

Parallels:
> Moon/Uranus, Sun/Mercury, Saturn/Pluto

Contraparallels:
> Jupiter/Neptune, Pluto/Mercury, Saturn/Mercury

Triangle elevation:
> Moon-Mars-Uranus

Exdek:
> Venus

Elevation by proximity:
> Pluto contraparallel Mercury

Eclipse:
> Sun/Mercury

Grand elevation:
> Mars (Mars conjunct Uranus, Saturn sextile Mars, Moon sextile Mars, Moon parallel Mars, Mars-Moon-Uranus triangle, Mars parallel Uranus)

The GPI of Henry's chart is 26, and the P/N is +1.00.

MATILDA

Matilda has been placed in a state mental institution on three separate occasions and has received four episodes of ECT. She has severe recurrent depression which has resulted in eight hospital admissions and trials of at least ten different psychotropic medications. Matilda has held jobs on an intermittent basis but her depression symptoms have always prevented her from maintaining stable employment.

Matilda's birth chart displays two of the highest-risk marker aspects for depression: Pluto/Mars parallel and Saturn/Pluto parallel. The Pluto/Mars parallel is also elevated by proximity. Her P/N is very low (-0.41), due to a large percentage of negative elevations

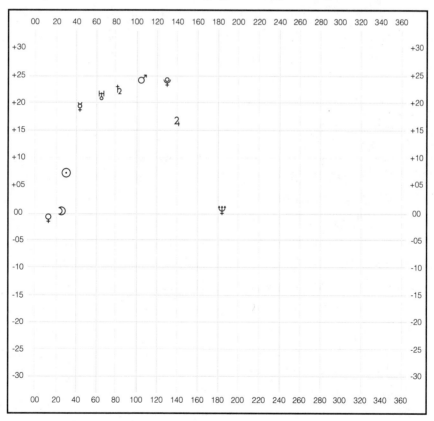

Chart 9: Matilda

in her chart. The triangle elevation involving Saturn-Pluto-Mars is frequently prominent in clients who have depression that is refractory to treatment.

Markers for Major Depression (11)

Trines:
Jupiter/Uranus, Uranus/Neptune

Parallels:
Pluto/Mars, Saturn/Pluto, Moon/Venus

Triangles:
Pluto-Mars-Saturn

Hidek:
Uranus

Exdek:
Mars

Proximity elevation:
Pluto/Mars parallel

Grand elevations:
1) Mars (Mercury sextile Mars, Pluto/Mars parallel, Saturn/Mars parallel, Pluto-Mars-Saturn triangle, Exdek Mars, Pluto/Mars parallel proximity elevation)
2) Pluto (Sun square Pluto, Pluto Mars parallel, Saturn parallel Pluto, Pluto-Mars-Saturn triangle, Exdek Pluto, Pluto/Mars parallel proximity elevation)

The GPI of Matilda's chart is 24, and the P/N is -0.41.

DENISE

Denise has a four-year history of recurrent depression. Since treatment began she has been stabilized on antidepressant medications, but each attempt to withdraw them has resulted in a return of her illness. However, despite her condition's chronic nature, Denise has held a job as an office manager for twelve years and has never been hospitalized.

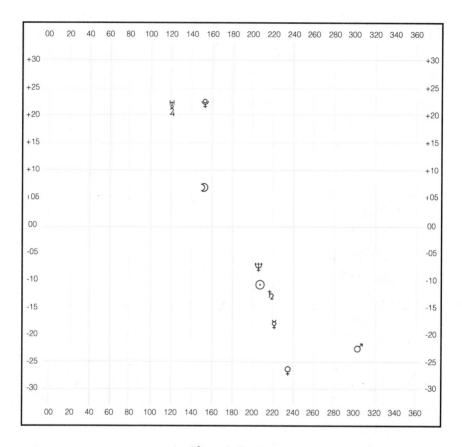

Chart 4: Denise

Denise's P/N is significantly more positive than that of Matilda or Henry, and she does not have either of the more dire marker aspects for depression in her birth chart—the Saturn/Pluto or Pluto/Mars parallel. However, she does have the Pluto/Mars con-traparallel and it is unfortunately elevated by proximity.

Her Grand Elevation of Mars consists of six positive eleva-tions and her Grand Elevation of Pluto consists of nine positive elevations. This intense focus of positive energy combined with a large positive P/N may have helped Denise escape the more severe consequences of her illness. Her Pluto and Mars are located in the area of high declination and this too may have helped mitigate their potentially negative effects of these two planets. Any planet located in the Hidek area experiences a decrease in its negative potential, with the exception of Saturn, the negative potential of which increases as its degree of declination increases. An Exdek Saturn is an exceptionally unfortunate aspect in a birth chart.

Markers for Major Depression (10)

Trines:
> Jupiter/Venus

Squares:
> Uranus/Neptune

Parallels:
> Pluto/Uranus

Contraparallels:
> Jupiter/Mercury

Hidek:
> Uranus, Pluto

Exdek:
> Venus

Proximity elevation:
> Pluto/Mars contraparallel

Grand elevations:
> 1) Mars (Venus/Mars sextile, Pluto/Mars contraparallel, Jupiter/Mars contraparallel, Uranus/Mars contraparallel, quad elevation [Pluto-Uranus-Jupiter-Mars], proximity elevation [Pluto/Mars contraparallel])
>
> 2) Pluto (Pluto/Neptune conjunction, Neptune/Pluto sextile, Sun/Pluto sextile, Pluto/Uranus parallel, Jupiter/Pluto parallel, Pluto/Mars contraparallel, quad elevation [Pluto-Uranus-Jupiter-Mars], Hidek Pluto, proximity elevation [Pluto contraparallel Mars])

The GPI for Denise's chart is 41 and the P/N is +1.73.

DAVID

David has a three-year history of depression. He has been fortunate in that he has been stabilized on the first antidepressant he tried and he has never been hospitalized. He is employed as an engineer.

Even though David has eleven marker aspects for major depression, he does not have the Saturn/Pluto parallel or the Pluto/ Mars parallel as seen in the first two test charts. His P/N is a very good +1.80 and his Pluto is located in the area of Hidek. He does have a longitudinal proximity elevation of Saturn/Pluto, and this may add to the chronicity of his disease. He also has the Pluto/Mercury parallel. Interestingly, this chart has the very rare Neptune/Mars eclipse.

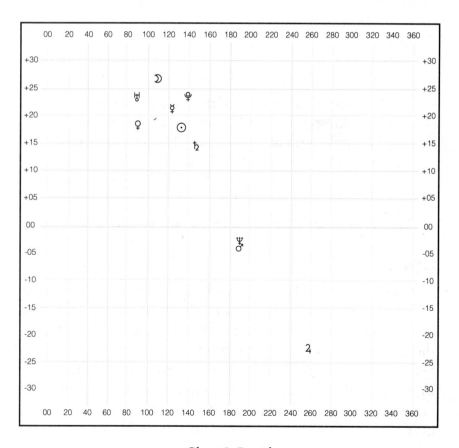

Chart 5: David

Markers for Major Depression (11)

Conjunctions:
    Venus/Uranus, Sun/Pluto

Trines:
    Jupiter/Pluto

Sextile:
    Sun/Neptune, Saturn/Uranus

Parallels:
    Pluto/Uranus

Contraparallels:
    Jupiter/Uranus, Jupiter/Mercury

Hidek:
    Pluto

Exdek:
    Moon

Grand elevation:
    Pluto (Sun/Pluto conjunction, Jupiter/Pluto trine,
       Pluto/Neptune sextile, Pluto/ Mercury parallel,
       Pluto/Uranus parallel, Jupiter/Pluto contraparallel,
       quad elevation [Jupiter-Pluto-Uranus-Mercury],
       Hidek Pluto, proximity elevation [Pluto/Uranus
       parallel])

The GPI for David's chart is 28 and the P/N is +1.80.

CYNTHIA

Cynthia experienced her first episode of depression at the tender age of eight when she attempted to kill herself by jumping from her parents' second-floor balcony. Following this suicide attempt, she was hospitalized for three weeks and started what was to become a lifelong relationship with the psychiatric community. By age seventeen Cynthia had tried to kill herself six times, and her desperate parents agreed to allow her doctors to administer ECT. After the ECT, she responded better to the antidepressant medication and psychotherapy but she continued to experience cyclic episodes of depression.

She married her first husband at age eighteen and soon became pregnant with her first child. Her depression returned during the last two months of the pregnancy, and she was hospitalized for her own protection. Following the delivery of her baby, her depression worsened and she was hospitalized for another episode of ECT.

Cynthia has been hospitalized a total of twenty-four times for the treatment of depression. She experiences an almost constant barrage of negative thoughts about herself and she feels that she is always depressed no matter what medication she tries or what new treatment process she goes through. She has been identified

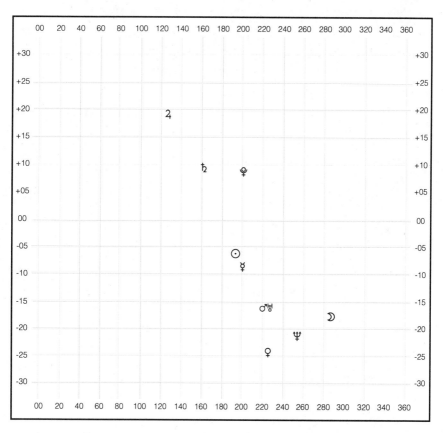

Chart 6: Cynthia

as a chronically mentally ill patient and she has applied for permanent disability benefits.

Cynthia's birth chart displays eleven marker aspects for depression. She has the Saturn/Pluto parallel, the Uranus/Moon parallel, and the Pluto/Mercury contraparallel, all of which form a deadly triad. These aspects, as we have seen in two previous birth charts, are associated with a high risk for the development of recurrent depression that can be refractory to treatment. She has a high number of marker aspects for depression, easily seen in the declinations and longitudes.

Other than the grand elevation of Saturn, the negative indicators in Cynthia's chart are not particularly strong. Her P/N is not excessively low (+1.18), but her GPI (24) is below average, which may mean that she has a large number of strong marker elevations relative to the total number of elevations in her chart. This may be an indicator of the strength of the Saturn, Mercury, and Pluto placements we find here. Further research is needed to ascertain the true importance of these placements in the charts of persons afflicted with this disorder.

Markers for Major Depression (18)

Conjunctions:
   Sun/Mercury

Sextiles:
   Sun/Neptune, Moon/Uranus, Saturn/Uranus

Squares:
   Moon/Mercury, Saturn/Neptune

Parallels:
   Saturn/Pluto, Sun/Mercury, Uranus/Moon

Contraparallels:
   Saturn/Mercury, Pluto/Mercury, Jupiter/Neptune

Triangle elevation:
   Mars-Uranus-Moon

Exdek:
   Venus

Proximity elevation:
   Pluto/Mercury contraparallel

Eclipse:
   Sun/Mercury

Grand elevation:
   Mars (Uranus/Mars conjunction, Moon/Mars sextile, Uranus/Mars parallel, Mars-Uranus-Moon triangle, Saturn/Mars sextile, Mars/Moon parallel)

The GPI of Cynthia's chart is 24 and the P/N is +1.18.

BETTY

Betty has been confined to a state hospital almost continuously since she was thirty-four years old. Each time a release into the community is attempted, she tries another serious suicide attempt. To date she has attempted suicide more than thirty times.

This chart provides an excellent example of the power of using declinations in astrology. The Saturn-Mars-Pluto triangle is visible quite clearly very high in the sky and is one of the clearest examples of a marker aspect for depression in a birth chart that I have ever seen.Again we see some familiar astrological predictors of chronic depression: Saturn/Pluto parallel, Pluto/Mars parallel, and a proximity enhancement of the Pluto/Mars parallel. Pluto and Mars are elevated by extreme declination, and therefore their negative energies are greatly expanded. This expansion is again enhanced by the proximity elevation shared by these two planets. In addition, both planets are simultaneously parallel to Saturn, a fact that adds even more greatly to their already extremely negative energies. Both Saturn and Mars are involved in negative grand elevations, and Pluto has a fifth degree negative elevation in this chart. These elevations contribute strongly to her low P/N.

Planetary eclipses are fairly common occurrences that demarcate areas of energy flux where we can see enormous changes in planetary potential. The powerful eclipse involving Saturn and Mars is one of the strongest influences in this chart. Since both

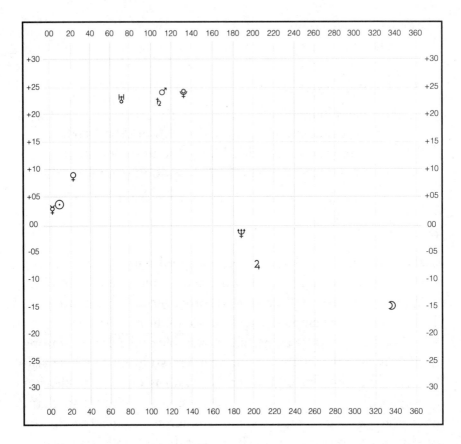

Chart 7: Betty

planets are involved in negative grand elevations, their expression will tend to dominate all other planetary energy patterns in the chart except those that are involved in positive grand elevations. In this case, the Sun is involved in a grand elevation, fortunately providing some balance to these forces.

Markers for Major Depression (10)
Conjunction:
   Sun/Mercury
Trine:
   Uranus/Neptune
Parallels:
   Pluto/Mars, Saturn/Pluto

Triangle elevation:
   Saturn-Pluto-Mars
Hidek:
   Uranus
Exdek:
   Mars
Proximity elevation:
   Pluto/Mars parallel
Eclipse:
   Sun/Mercury
Grand elevation:
   Sun (Sun/Mercury conjunction, Sun/Uranus sextile,
   Sun/Mercury parallel, Sun/Neptune contraparallel,
   triangle elevation [Sun-Mercury-Neptune],
   Sun/Pluto trine

The GPI of Betty's chart is 29 and the P/N is -0.611.

Exdek Mars

Extreme elevation enhancements are considered to be negative because they occur in areas of the chart where planetary energies tend to become erratic. Five of the eighteen charts in the depression test group displayed Mars elevations by extreme declination. My research has revealed that Exdek Mars elevations tend to be associated with an increase in suicidal/homicidal behaviors. Additional elevations of Exdek Mars by Saturn, Venus, Neptune, or Pluto tend to exacerbate the behaviors. Exdek eclipses involving Mars, Saturn, Venus, Neptune or Pluto are particularly problematic and they denote times when suicidal/homicidal behaviors tend to increase.

Conclusions

From the above data, I conclude that there are indeed certain planetary markers associated with an increased astrological risk for the development of depression. The root cause of this is not clear, but it is my hope that other astrologers will use these signs in their work with depressed patients in order to improve our understanding of this phenomenon. I will further discuss the possible ramifications of the data presented here in later chapters.

High Risk Transits for Major Depression

When the following conditions involving transiting planets occur, persons who exhibit signs of Major Depression can experience an intensification of symptoms.

- Saturn/Pluto parallel
- Pluto/Mars parallel
- Jupiter/Neptune contraparallel
- Exdek Mars
- Saturn/Neptune square
- Saturn/Uranus square

---

7   Anxiety Disorders

ANXIETY DISORDERS ARE THE MOST COMMON TYPE OF PSYCHIATRIC disorders, accounting for 32% of the total mental health expenditures in the United States. There are five types of anxiety disorders:

- Panic disorder
- Phobic disorder
- Obsessive-compulsive disorder
- Post-traumatic stress disorder
- Generalized anxiety disorder

Panic disorder is characterized by spontaneous panic attacks and may be associated with agoraphobia (fear of being in open spaces, outside the home alone, or in a crowd). Agoraphobia can occur alone, but these patients usually have associated panic attacks.

Phobic disorder is marked by an irrational fear of an object or situation and the need to avoid it. This may include a fear of public speaking, fear of water, fear of animals, etc.

Obsessive-compulsive disorder is characterized by recurrent intrusive ideas, impulses, thoughts, and/or resulting patterns of behavior that produce anxiety if resisted.

Post-traumatic stress disorder is characterized by anxiety connected to an event or group of events that result in extraordinary major life stress. The traumatic event is relived in dreams and waking thoughts.

Generalized anxiety disorder is characterized by chronic, generalized anxiety for at least a full month's duration. The patient experiences a multifocal state of fear, and the condition may also be accompanied by a number of physiological symptoms.

For the purposes of this study, we examined the charts of patients with a diagnosis of panic disorder, obsessive-compulsive disorder, or generalized anxiety disorder. We will now take a closer look at these three types of anxiety disorders.

PANIC DISORDER

Panic disorder affects 2 to 4% of the general population. The typical age of onset is the late twenties, and the disorder tends to run in families. Men and women tend to have an equal incidence of panic disorder without agoraphobia, but women have a higher incidence of panic disorder with agoraphobia. Panic disorder patients are also at increased risk for the development of major depression. Listed below are the DSM-IV criteria for panic disorder with agoraphobia.

- At some time during the disturbance, one or more panic attacks (periods of intense fear or discomfort) have occurred that were unexpected—i.e., did not occur immediately before or upon exposure to a situation that typically caused anxiety—and were not triggered by situations in which the person was the focus of others' attention
- At least four of the following symptoms developed during at least one of the attacks:
    1) Shortness of breath or smothering sensations
    2) Dizziness, unsteady feelings, or faintness
    3) Palpitations or accelerated heart rate
    4) Trembling or shaking
    5) Sweating
    6) Choking
    7) Nausea or abdominal distress
    8) Depersonalization or derealization
    9) Numbness or tingling sensations

10) Flushes (hot flashes) or chills

11) Chest pain or discomfort

12) Fear of dying

13) Fear of going crazy or of loss of control

The criteria for panic disorder with agoraphobia include the above, but adds one or more of these symptoms of agoraphobia:

- Fear of being in open spaces or situations from which escape might be difficult

- Restricting travel or needing a companion when away from home

- Enduring agoraphobic situations with intense anxiety*

The most common fears reported by panic disorder patients include fear of driving, fear of malls, fear of being alone, fear of crowds, and fear of leaving home. Panic attacks strike out of the blue and last anywhere from several minutes to over one hour. Patients suffering from panic attacks are often convinced that they are dying or that the attack is indicative of a life-threatening medical condition. However, panic attacks are rarely fatal and respond well to appropriate treatment. A combination of insight-oriented psychotherapy, meditation, and medication management yields a very high remission for the disorder. Anxiolytic medications such as those prescribed under the brand names Valium, Xanax, and Klonopin are commonly used in the treatment of this condition.

Theories concerning the cause of panic disorder are numerous. Psychoanalytic theory proposes that panic attacks are produced by unconscious impulses—e.g., sex, aggression—which threaten to enter the conscious mind and produce anxiety. Unconscious defense mechanisms are used to ward off anxiety but instead produce phobias, compulsions, and panic attacks. Learning theory suggests that anxiety is produced by frustration or stress that is learned through identification. Anxiety disorders are associated with a prolapse of the heart's mitral valve in 50% of patients. The causative mechanism of this association is unknown.

* Reprinted with permission from the Diagnostic and Statistical Manual of Mental Disorders, Fourth Edition. Copyright 1994 American Psychiatric Association.

Some medical conditions may cause anxiety. These include vitamin B deficiency, hypoglycemia, premenstrual syndrome, lupus erythematous, hypothyroidism, and migraine headaches. PET (positron emission tomography) scans show decreased metabolism in the orbital gyrus, caudate nuclei, and in the cingulate gyrus. PET scans also reveal increased blood flow in the frontal lobe when the patient experiences anxiety.

In general, the specific mechanism of the cause of panic attacks is unknown. However, patients who suffer from panic attacks are more susceptible to lactic acid infusion-induced panic attacks than control patients.

OBSESSIVE-COMPULSIVE DISORDER

Obsessive-compulsive disorder (OCD) is characterized by involuntary thoughts, ideas, urges, impulses or worries that run though one's mind and purposeless repetitive behaviors. The disorder affects 2.5% of the U.S. population. It can strike men, women, children, and people of all age, ethnic, and socioeconomic groups. OCD is considered to occur when these feelings are experienced for more than one hour each day in a way that interferes with one's life.

The disorder generally begins during childhood or young adulthood. Common obsessions include fear of contamination, fixation on lucky numbers, excessive doubt, and fear of danger to self or others. Trying to ignore these things causes extreme anxiety. Compulsions include repetitive rituals such as hand washing, counting, checking, hoarding, or arranging. A feeling exists that these rituals must be performed or something bad will happen. OCD might result from a chemical imbalance and appears to have a strong genetic factor. Medication and psychotherapy have proven to be effective in reducing obsessive thoughts and compulsive behavior. Most people treated with effective medications find their symptoms reduced by about half.

GENERALIZED ANXIETY DISORDER

Generalized anxiety disorder is characterized by chronic, generalized anxiety for at least a full month's duration. Other symptoms include motor tension (trembling, twitching, aches, soreness, restlessness, and fatigue), autonomic hyperactivity (shortness of breath, dry mouth, nausea, diarrhea, or other abdominal distress, flushes, frequent urination, trouble swallowing, sweating, irritability, insomnia, and an exaggerated startle response).

STUDY 2: ANXIETY DISORDER

All of the patients in the anxiety test group for this study have a diagnosis of panic disorder, generalized anxiety disorder, or obsessive-compulsive disorder. In this study, the test charts of ten patients who had at least a one-year history of clinical depression were analyzed and contrasted with the control group. The resulting astrological markers are presented below and in Graph 4 (see page 80).

Planetary Indices	Test Group	Control Group	(Change)
Sun	+117	+181	-35%
Moon	-55	+112	-203%
Mercury	-95	+170	-178%
Venus	+165	+133	+19.4%
Mars	-655	-450	-31%
Jupiter	+126	+194	-35%
Saturn	-600	-604	+1%
Uranus	+139	+137	+1.4%
Neptune	+126	+148	-15%
Pluto	+150	+112	+25%

Specific Markers for Anxiety Disorder (13)

Conjunctions:
Venus/Mars, Saturn/Pluto

Sextile:
Sun/Pluto

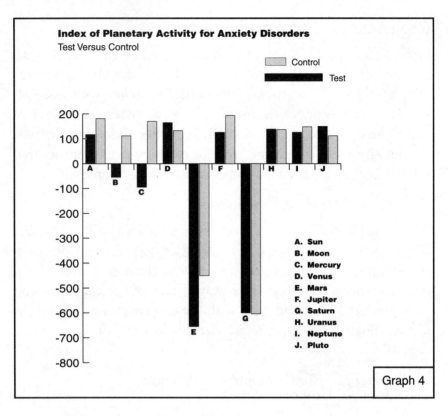

Index of Planetary Activity for Anxiety Disorders
Test Versus Control

Control
Test

A. Sun
B. Moon
C. Mercury
D. Venus
E. Mars
F. Jupiter
G. Saturn
H. Uranus
I. Neptune
J. Pluto

Graph 4

Parallels:
  Jupiter/Mercury, Saturn/Mercury, Pluto/Venus,
  Uranus/Venus

Contraparallel:
  Sun/Neptune

Hidek:
  Sun

Exdek:
  Mercury

Eclipse:
  Venus/Mars

Grand elevations:
  Sun, Venus

The GPI of the test group is 31.6, and the P/N is -0.904

Graph 5 reveals a greater than threefold increase in the average number of anxiety disorder marker aspects per chart when compared to the control charts.

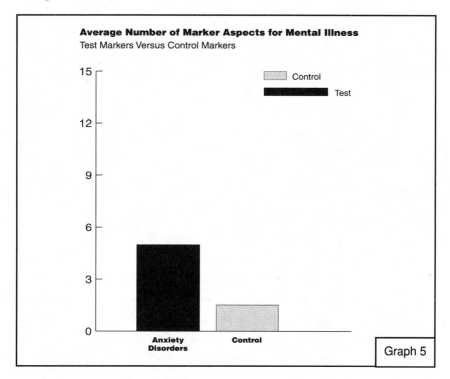

Graph 5

Overall, anxiety disorder does display some readily identifiable astrological marker aspects. The birth charts of these patients tend to be more active than average, to have a lower P/N, and an above-average number of planets in the Exdek regions. The Venus/Mars eclipse is also a prominent associated sign. The charts are characterized by a high degree of negative Mercury activity, which may destabilize the nascent presentation of this planet's otherwise controlled energies.

In particular, five out of ten of the test group patients had birth charts which displayed Exdek Mercury. Mercury is the planet associated with the nervous system and is closely linked with the conscious mind. Planetary energies tend to become erratic in the Exdek area, and an erratic manifestation of Mercury's energy might well be associated with an uncontrolled and unpredictable release of energy from within the nervous system.

There was also a strong downward shift in the Moon's planetary index for this test group when compared to the control group. This shift in planetary forces may astrologically provide a supportive function for the panic process. However, elevations involving the Moon do not figure prominently in the marker aspects.

The following four examples present the histories and charts of patients who display a large number of signs of anxiety disorder. All names used to identify the patients are pseudonyms.

DANIEL

Daniel experienced his first panic attack three years ago. He was driving home after a long day at work when he came upon a new overpass that he had never driven across. As he neared the center of the overpass, he noticed that he was breathing heavily and that his heart rate was very fast. When he reached the end of the overpass he pulled over, got out of the car and began gasping for air. He was sure that he was going to die or pass out. Nauseating waves of intense anxiety swept over him for almost thirty minutes before he regained control.

Two weeks later, he experienced a similar episode while shopping at the mall. At the end of three months he had experienced more than twenty of these attacks in a variety of places. They seemed to come from nowhere and lasted anywhere from a few minutes to a full hour. He began to isolate himself and only went out to go to work. Finally, his wife convinced him to seek help.

He was diagnosed with panic disorder with agoraphobia, placed on medication, and completed several counseling sessions. For the first time in months, he began to feel that he was returning to his normal self. Six months later he stopped the medication on his own and canceled his therapy sessions. Within two weeks, his panic attacks returned and he began a cycle of exacerbation and remission which has continued for the last three years.

Daniel's birth chart prominently displays several important signs of panic disorder, including five grand elevations, two quads, one eclipse, and three Exdek planets, including Mercury. All of the grand elevations were positive (Sun, Mercury, Venus, Uranus, and Pluto). This configuration of tremendous planetary force combined with the opposite pull of three Exdek elevations may create a maelstrom of conflicting planetary forces that could also contribute to the process of the formation of panic disorders.

Markers for Anxiety Disorder (8)

Conjunction:
  Saturn/Pluto

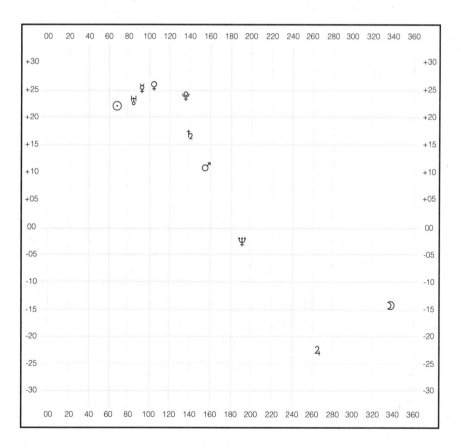

Chart 8: Daniel

Sextile:
    Sun/Pluto
Parallels:
    Venus/Uranus, Venus/Pluto
Hidek:
    Sun
Exdek:
    Mercury
Grand elevations:
    1) Sun: (Sun/Neptune trine, Sun/Pluto sextile,
    Sun/Pluto parallel, Sun/Uranus parallel, Sun/Jupiter
    contraparallel, Quad elevation [Sun-Jupiter-Uranus-
    Pluto], Hidek Sun)

    2) Venus: (Moon/Venus trine, Venus/Mars sextile,
    Mercury/Venus parallel, Venus/Pluto parallel,
    Venus/Uranus parallel, Quad elevation [Mercury-
    Uranus-Pluto-Venus], Proximity elevation [Mercury
    parallel Venus])

The GPI for Daniel's chart is 37 and the P/N is 2.08.

HILARY

Eighteen months ago, Hilary experienced her first panic attack, just as she finished signing the closing papers for a big marketing deal she had been working on for six months. Before her clients could leave the office, she noticed that her hands were sweating profusely and that her heart rate was fast. She felt faint and for a moment she thought that she might throw up. She initially thought that something she had eaten at lunch had not agreed with her. She quickly ushered her clients out of the room with embarrassed apologies and rushed to the bathroom.

Minutes later, rapid episodes of hot flashes, chills, and severe chest pain began. She called 911 and reported that she felt that she was having a heart attack. Twelve hours later, after a thorough medical evaluation had ruled out heart disease as a cause for her symptoms, she went home and called in sick for the next day.

She did not experience another attack for two weeks. Then suddenly, during a party for one of her closest friends, she began shaking uncontrollably and felt that she was choking. Sweat ran down her face profusely and she was intensely short of breath. Her friends called an ambulance, and ten hours later a heart attack was ruled out once again.

Hilary experienced six more episodes over the next eight months before her family physician suggested that she consult a psychiatrist, who gave her a diagnosis of panic disorder without agoraphobia. She was started on medication and was given training in relaxation techniques. Within two weeks, her attacks

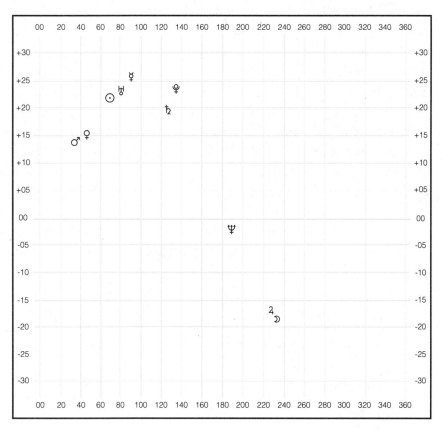

Chart 9: Hilary

stopped and she resumed her normal routine. Eight months later, the medication was phased out over a period of six weeks. Within ten days the panic attacks returned and she was placed back on the medication.

Hilary's story is not unusual for a person suffering from panic disorder. In medical circles, panic disorder is called the "great mimic" because its presentation resembles so many different medical conditions. Generally, most patients consult a psychiatrist only after they have endured a battery of medical tests and examinations designed to rule out other illnesses.

Hilary's birth chart displays a number of familiar astrological signs that are associated with an anxiety disorder. She has a very prominent Exdek Mercury (which we also saw in the preceding chart), a Saturn/Pluto conjunction, a Venus/Mars conjunction, and a Sun/Pluto sextile.

The Venus/Mars conjunction helps to form a Venus/Mars eclipse, which is another marker aspect associated with anxiety disorders. This eclipse, combined with the opposing yet powerful positive and negative aspects of Pluto, may create a great deal of planetary tension within this birth chart. The Venus/Mars eclipse is powerful because it combines the power of two planets which are within close proximity to the Earth relative to the other planets, and because their energies are even more tightly focused when they are in eclipsing positions to each other.

In addition, Pluto (associated with the latent forces of the deep unconscious) is parallel to Exdek Mercury. This combination may serve to awaken this archetypal giant.

Markers for Anxiety Disorder (5)

Conjunctions:
   Venus/Mars, Saturn/Pluto

Sextile:
   Sun/Pluto

Exdek:
   Mercury

Eclipse:
Venus/Mars

The GPI of Hilary's chart is 27 and the P/N is +1.25.

CATHERINE

Catherine was first given the diagnosis of panic disorder with agoraphobia when she was thirty. She was started on Xanax by her family physician and was eventually stabilized on a three-times-per-day dosing schedule. Despite her treatment, she continues to be immobilized by her attacks and cannot leave her home without her companion. She has not been able to work for several years.

Catherine's chart prominently displays several familiar signs associated with anxiety disorders. Once again we see the Sun/Pluto sextile, Exdek Mercury, and grand elevations involving the Sun and Venus. Catherine's chart has a very low negative P/N and an above-average GPI. This is indicative of significant astrological strain among the planetary forces.

The Hidek Saturn quad adds colossal tension to this chart. Much of the reason for the low P/N in her chart rests with the fact that the Sun/Saturn parallel cancels out the positive balance normally provided by the Sun's presence in the Hidek position.

Hilary's chart also has six negative grand elevations: Sun, Venus, Saturn, Uranus, Pluto, and Mercury. This is an extraordinary accumulation of negative planetary energy. Five of these planets are involved in a very rare plenary elevation which is also elevated by high declination. Plenary elevations tend to place strain on the birth chart because of the sheer magnitude of the forces involved in creating and sustaining such a rare celestial event. In this particular chart, the valence of the entire elevation is negative because the Sun and Pluto are parallel to Saturn. Any planet involved in an aspect with Saturn will possess a negative value for all its declinational aspects.

High strain patterns within a chart—i.e., low negative P/N combined with a high GPI, high Saturn index, and a large number

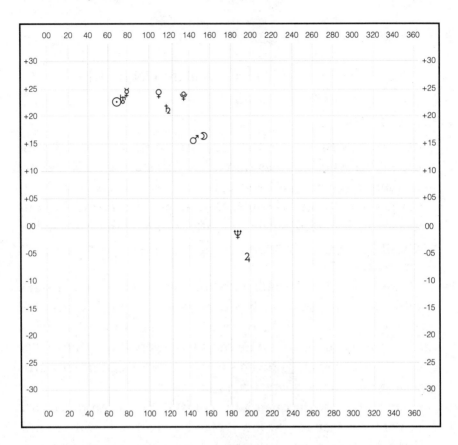

Chart 10: Catherine

of planets in the Exdek position—are often associated with disabling conditions, as seen in Catherine's case.

Marker Aspects for Anxiety Disorder (7)

Sextile:
   Sun/Pluto

Parallels:
   Venus/Uranus, Venus/Pluto

Hidek:
   Sun

Exdek:
   Mercury

Grand elevations:

    1) Sun (Sun/Uranus parallel, Sun/Mercury parallel, Sun/Venus parallel, Sun/Pluto parallel, Sun/Saturn parallel, Quad elevation [Sun-Saturn-Uranus-Pluto], Plenary elevation [Sun-Uranus-Mercury-Venus-Pluto], Hidek Sun)

    2) Venus (Venus/Jupiter square, Sun/Venus parallel, Venus/Uranus parallel, Venus/Pluto parallel, Plenary elevation [Sun-Uranus-Mercury-Venus-Pluto], Exdek Venus, Proximity elevation [Mercury/Venus parallel])

The GPI for Catherine's chart is 38 and the P/N is -0.42.

PONCE

Ponce was diagnosed with severe obsessive-compulsive disorder ten years ago. Ponce washes his hands more than thirty times per day, despite the resulting open, weeping cuts he bears on both hands. He cannot leave his home without checking the doors at least twelve times. His shirts must be arranged in order of the date of purchase or he cannot put one on. He counts license plate numbers looking for specific number patterns even though he knows this habit is irrational and illogical. Attempts to stop these behaviors only worsen his anxiety. Ponce has taken medication intermittently to control these symptoms, but prefers to try to master the problem on his own.

Ponce's birth chart displays the highest number of marker aspects associated with the anxiety disorders of all the test group charts. Among the more prominent markers are the Venus/Mars conjunction, Hidek Sun, Venus/Mars eclipse, and grand elevations of the Sun and Venus. Ponce has a fourth-degree negative Mercury and two very strong negative parallels involving Mercury— Jupiter/Mercury and Saturn/Mercury. He also has four triangle elevations, a planetary quad, two proximity elevations, two eclipses, and six grand elevations.

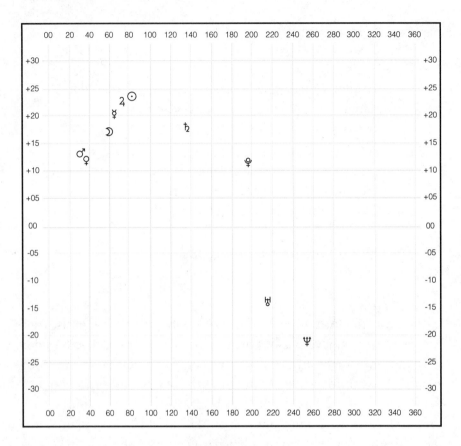

Chart 11: Ponce

Fortunately, his P/N is a very positive +1.71 when one considers his above-average GPI of 38. Therefore, even though he possesses a very active, very complex, and potentially very problematic birth chart, the combination of planetary forces within his chart is ultimately quite manageable. Indeed, if Ponce chose to complete a good treatment program for his illness, he would greatly enhance his quality of life.

Marker Aspects for Anxiety Disorder (9)

Conjunction:
     Venus/Mars

Parallels:
Jupiter/Mercury, Saturn/Mercury, Pluto/Venus

Contraparallel:
Sun/Neptune

Hidek:
Sun

Eclipse:
Venus/Mars

Grand elevations:

1) Sun (Sun/Jupiter conjunction, Sun/Jupiter parallel, Sun/Neptune contraparallel, Triangle elevations [Sun-Jupiter-Neptune; Sun-Jupiter-Mercury], Hidek Sun)

2) Venus (Venus/Mars conjunction, Mars/Venus parallel, Uranus/Venus contraparallel, Triangle elevation [Pluto-Venus-Mars], Quad elevation [Uranus-Pluto-Venus-Mars], Proximity elevation [Pluto/Venus parallel, Pluto/Venus parallel]).

The GPI of Ponce's chart is 38 and the P/N is +1.71.

High-Risk Transits for Anxiety Disorder

When the following conditions involving transiting planets occur, persons who exhibit signs of Anxiety Disorder can experience an intensification of symptoms.

- **Jupiter/Mercury parallel**
- **Saturn/Mercury parallel**
- **Pluto/Venus parallel**
- **Exdek Mercury**
- **Venus/Mars conjunction**

8   Schizophrenia

SCHIZOPHRENIA IS ONE OF THE MOST WIDELY KNOWN AND PERHAPS the most mysterious of all the mental illnesses. It is characterized by psychotic symptoms that severely impair the ability to function. The disorder was first described by Belgian psychiatrist Benedict Morel in 1852. He called it *demence precoce.* In 1896, Emil Kraeplin, a German psychiatrist, coined the term *dementia praecox,* describing a group of illnesses that typically began during adolescence and progressed into dementia. In 1911 Swiss psychiatrist Eugen Bleuler coined the term *schizophrenia.*

Two million Americans suffer from schizophrenia and one in 100 is hospitalized at some time for it. Worldwide, two million new cases appear each year. The disease strikes men and women at an equal rate and the most common ages of onset are between fifteen and thirty-five. Worldwide studies reveal a disproportionate number of schizophrenic persons born during the winter months.

No single cause of schizophrenia has been identified. There appears to be a genetic component. Persons with first-degree relatives, who have two schizophrenic parents, and/or who are identical or fraternal twins are at greatly increased risk.

Some scientists believe that the illness is caused by a slow virus. The increased incidence of perinatal complications and seasonality seem to support this theory. Brain imaging (CT) scans show cortical atrophy in 10 to 35% of patients, enlargement of the lateral and third ventricle in 10 to 50% of patients; and atrophy of the cerebellum. Patients who display CT scan changes in the brain who are affected by schizophrenia seem to have a poorer prognosis. There is a decline in IQ as the disease progresses. There are a number of neurological changes which can be seen in schizophrenic patients through electroencephalogram (EEG) testing, evoked potential (EP) studies, immunologic studies, and endocrine studies.

Schizophrenia is treated by a combination of medication, psychotherapy, intermittent hospitalization, and community support. Episodes may be triggered by emotional trauma, drugs, and separations. Over time, the course of schizophrenia is characterized by a gradual mental decline. Roughly one-third of patients lead somewhat normal lives, one-third continue to experience symptoms but are able to function within society, and one-third may be markedly impaired and require frequent hospitalization.

Schizophrenia is diagnosed by use of a cluster of symptoms. The DSM-IV criteria are most widely used and accepted. Symptoms of the disorder must be continuously present for at least six months, and the diagnosis of schizophrenia cannot be associated with a disturbance in mood, or the use of drugs or alcohol. The signs and symptoms of schizophrenia are:

- Impaired overall functioning
- Abnormal thought content (delusions, poverty of content)
- Illogical form of thought (loosening of associations, overinclusiveness, tangentiality, incoherence)
- Distorted perception (visual, smell, touch, and/or auditory hallucinations)
- Changed affect (flat, blunted, silly, labile)
- Impaired sense of self (gender confusion, inability to distinguish internal from external reality)
- Altered volition (marked ambivalence, inadequate drive)
- Impaired social function (social withdrawal, emotional detachment, aggressiveness, sexual inappropriateness)
- Change in psychomotor functioning (agitation, grimacing, rituals, posturing)
- Change in sensorium (orientation to time, place, and person)

There are considered to be three major phases in the development of schizophrenia:

- Prodromal, in which there is a clear decline in functioning before the active phase of the disease
- Active, in which major symptoms of the disorder occur
- Remission, which is characterized by a marked reduction in the number of presenting symptoms, and at the height of which the person with a history of schizophrenia is free of all symptoms, whether or not on medication.*

The five primary classifications of schizophrenia are: *Catatonic, Disorganized, Paranoid, Undifferentiated,* and *Residual.* Each is characterized by specific signs and symptoms.

STUDY 3: SCHIZOPHRENIA

Fourteen schizophrenic patients with at least a two-year history of active treatment were included in the following study. All met DSM-IV criteria for either the Disorganized, Paranoid, or Undifferentiated type of schizophrenia. The marker aspects are listed below, contrasted with the control group.

Planetary Indices	Test Group	Control Group	(Change)
Sun	+133	+181	-26.6%
Moon	+150	+112	+25.3%
Mercury	+132	+170	-21.8%
Venus	+123	+133	-7.5%
Mars	-169	-450	+266%
Jupiter	+300	+194	+64.7%
Saturn	-564	-604	+6.7%
Uranus	+176	+137	+22.2%
Neptune	+152	+148	+2.6%
Pluto	+189	+112	+40.7%

* Reprinted with permission from the Diagnostic and Statistical Manual of Mental Disorders, Fourth Edition. Copyright 1994 American Psychiatric Association.

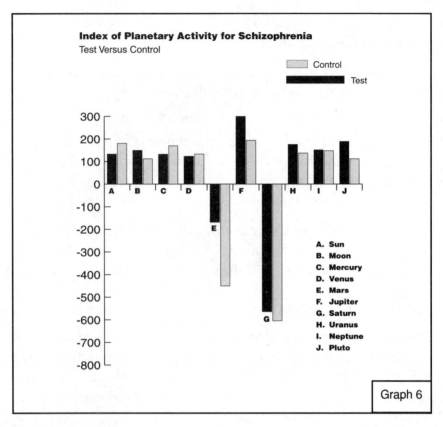

Index of Planetary Activity for Schizophrenia
Test Versus Control

Graph 6

A. Sun
B. Moon
C. Mercury
D. Venus
E. Mars
F. Jupiter
G. Saturn
H. Uranus
I. Neptune
J. Pluto

Specific Markers for Schizophrenia (22)

Conjunction:
    Mercury/Venus

Trines:
    Neptune/Mars, Saturn/Moon

Sextiles:
    Mars/Moon, Mars/Venus

Squares:
    Uranus/Neptune, Sun/Mars, Venus/Uranus

Oppositions:
    Pluto/Mars

Parallels:
    Sun/Mercury, Moon/Neptune, Venus/Mercury,
    Jupiter/Uranus, Sun/Venus

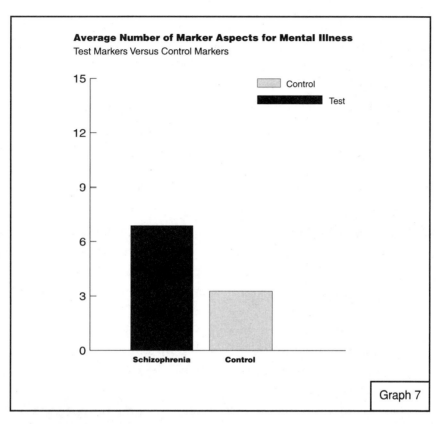

Average Number of Marker Aspects for Mental Illness
Test Markers Versus Control Markers

Graph 7

Contraparallels:
   Pluto/Mercury, Sun/Pluto
Hidek:
   Sun, Pluto
Proximity elevations:
   Jupiter/Uranus parallel
Grand elevations:
   Sun, Moon, Mercury

According to the results of this study, the astrological markers for schizophrenia occur at a much higher rate in the test group than in the controls. The placement and valence of the markers may indicate that the process of schizophrenia is associated with an overstimulation of the deep unconscious by high order planetary forces. This may result in a compensatory redirection of the errant forces into conscious energy patterns which ultimately organize themselves into delusional patterns of thought and behavior. High order elevations involving the Sun, Mercury, and Pluto, greatly above average Jupiter and Mars indexes, a negative P/N and an above average GPI are common markers for schizophrenia in the birth chart.

ERICH

Erich believes that a two-and-a-half-inch tall blue man lives within his brain. Unfortunately, Erich believes that this man is a demon. Six years ago, Erich was a successful architect with a large firm. He had recently graduated from college with honors, married his college sweetheart, and settled down in a suburban townhome in Scottsdale. The voices started one day while he was driving home. The man introduced himself as "The Bald One" and proceeded to explain to Erich how he was going to change his life for the worse. Erich initially thought that this voice was a figment of his imagination or perhaps a machination created by overwork and lack of exercise. He was wrong.

His wife noticed that he spent increasing amounts of time talking softly to himself and he seemed to be somewhat more distant. Erich felt tortured inside by the curses and slurs hurled at him by the little man. After several months of gradually increasing torture and insomnia, his wife convinced him to see his family physician.

His family doctor decided that Erich was suffering from stress and overwork and suggested that he take some time off. He took a three-week vacation with his wife to Puerto Rico which seemed to help for a time, but the voices returned a few weeks after the vacation and gradually proceeded to permeate all his waking hours. They threatened to kill him and his wife if he did not carry out bizarre rituals. He was also told to stop bathing and to run naked around his home seven times daily. When he was caught running around the home by the neighbors' children he was hospitalized.

During the hospitalization, Erich told his doctors about the little man. Despite their numerous arguments to the contrary, as well as three expertly done X-rays of his skull, they could not convince him that the little man was anything more than a delusion. Erich was placed on antipsychotic medication and advised to continue it until further notice. The medicine stopped the voices. After two months, Erich stopped the medication on his own and within weeks he relapsed into a state of psychosis. He lost his job because he became paranoid that his coworkers were conspiring to steal his thoughts and sell them to the company's competitors. He made a formal protest to his supervisor via the office PA system and had to be escorted from the building. Erich has been given a diagnosis of paranoid schizophrenia.

Erich's birth chart displays nine markers for schizophrenia. Sun square Mars can be a very energizing and potentially irritating

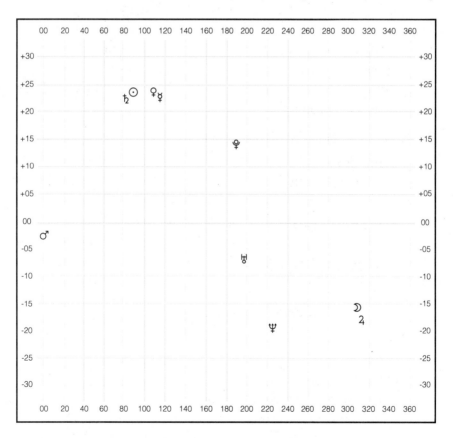

Chart 12: Erich

transit. In this case, its association with the Uranus/Venus square, the Sun/Venus and Sun/Mercury parallels, the Quad elevations involving the Sun, and the Hidek Sun elevation all may well combine to greatly overstimulate the patient's psyche.

Erich has a high order negative grand elevation of the Sun and a P/N of -0.381. He also has negative grand elevations of Venus, Saturn, and Mercury. Two of the eclipses in this chart are located in the Hidek area. These factors impart a large amount of negative potential to Erich's unconscious.

Erich has a fourth-degree elevation of Jupiter as well as a fifth-degree elevation of Mars. The most active planets in the schizophrenia test group are Jupiter and Mars. This unconscious expansion of aggressive energies is a common theme in the schizophrenic's profile. In Erich's case, this aggression ultimately became all-consuming and disabling. The little man may have been a conscious materialization of this overwhelming cacophony of negative unconscious mind potential. A negative P/N combined with multiple negative grand elevations in this chart does not bode well for Erich's prognosis.

Marker Aspects for Schizophrenia (9)

Conjunction:
   Mercury/Venus
Trine:
   Neptune/Mars
Squares:
   Sun/Mars, Uranus/Venus
Parallels:
   Sun/Venus, Sun/Mercury
Hidek:
   Sun
Grand elevations:
   1) Sun (Sun/Saturn trine, Sun/Mars square, Uranus/Venus square, Sun/Venus parallel, Sun/Mercury parallel, Hidek Sun, Sun/Saturn parallel, Quad

elevation [Saturn-Sun-Venus-Mercury], Proximity elevation [Sun/Venus parallel, Sun/Pluto square])

2) Mercury (Mercury/Mars trine, Neptune/Mars trine, Mercury/Uranus square, Saturn/Mercury parallel, Sun/Mercury parallel, Quad elevation [Saturn-Venus-Sun-Mercury], Hidek Mercury)

The GPI in Erich's chart is 29 and the P/N is -0.38.

ARTHUR

Arthur was diagnosed with undifferentiated schizophrenia three years ago. He hears voices, believes that he is a messenger from the far future sent back into the past by a giant race of benevolent moths, and disappears for days at a time. Between episodes of his illness, Arthur experiences complete remissions and is able to hold down a full-time job. His boss has a son who also has a diagnosis of schizophrenia and consequently he allows Arthur to return to work provided that he continues taking his medication.

Arthur's birth chart has ten signs that point to a predisposition to the development of schizophrenia. He was born in December, a winter month. His birth chart indicates a higher than average P/N of +1.69 and a very high GPI of 35.

Once again we see the Neptune/Mars trine and the Uranus/Neptune square as part of his marker aspect profile. Neptune is associated with the unconscious mind and stimulation by Mars or Uranus would probably serve to activate the latent energies therein in some unpredictable and unusual ways. He also has a high order (nine or more +/- elevations) grand elevation of Pluto. Pluto is associated with the collective unconscious and also with the deeper forces that impel the workings of the inner mind. Fortunately, the aspects which make up the grand elevation in this case are positive.

Arthur's auditory hallucinations are benign and rarely threaten him in any way. They are, however, overwhelming when they arise and their overall impetus is insurmountable once activated. This may be related to the abundance of positive aspects with a total of five positive grand elevations in his chart.

Astrologically, schizophrenia is often characterized by an over-abundance of psychic force which ultimately aggregates itself into some manner of systematized delusional thought or behavior pattern. This often creates dire consequences for the native, as in Arthur's case. The combined impetus of this symphony of aggregating forces may create a materialization of psychic force that organizes itself into a system of delusions and hallucinations. The protective influence of the positive valence of Arthur's aspects may also provide an overwhelming amount of animation to his thought processes, and the double proximity elevations involving Pluto may only heighten this process. The grand elevation of the Moon also signals an astrological heightening of the forces within Arthur's personal unconscious.

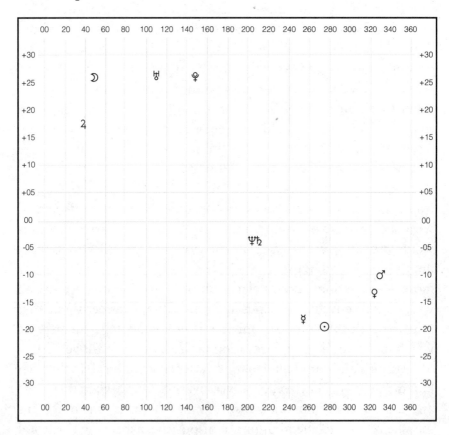

Chart 13: Arthur

Marker Aspects for Schizophrenia (10)

Trine:
Neptune/Mars

Square:
Uranus/Neptune

Parallels:
Sun/Mercury

Contraparallels:
Pluto/Mercury, Sun/Pluto

Hidek:
Sun, Pluto

Grand elevations:

1) Sun (Sun/Jupiter trine, Sun/Mercury parallel, Moon/Sun contraparallel, Uranus/Sun contraparallel, Pluto/Sun contraparallel, Plenary elevation [Sun-Moon-Uranus-Pluto- Mercury, Hidek Sun])

2) Moon (Moon/Uranus sextile, Jupiter/Moon longitudinal proximity elevation, Uranus/Moon parallel, Pluto/Moon parallel, Moon/Mercury contraparallel, Moon/Sun contraparallel, Plenary elevation [Sun-Moon-Uranus-Pluto-Mercury], Hidek Moon, proximity elevations, Pluto/Moon parallel, Uranus/Moon parallel)

3) Mercury (Mercury/Venus sextile, Sun/Mercury parallel, Moon/Mercury contraparallel, Uranus/Mercury contraparallel, Pluto/Mercury contraparallel, Hidek Mercury, Plenary elevation [Sun-Mercury-Moon-Uranus-Pluto])

The GPI of Arthur's chart is 35 and the P/N is +1.69.

FRANCES

Frances was given the diagnosis of paranoid schizophrenia when she was twenty-one years old. Since that time she has heard voices that tell her that she is a special representative of God and that she possesses extraordinary powers. Frances cannot demonstrate her powers nor can she describe them, she only knows that she has them. She has been in treatment for schizophrenia for more than ten years. As long as she takes her medication, she is able to function in her job. She has been able to maintain a family, successfully taking care of her four children.

Frances' birth chart displays fourteen marker aspects that demonstrate a predisposition toward the development of schizophrenia. Interestingly, Frances was also born in the middle of winter. As we have seen in previous charts in this test group, she has the Uranus/Neptune square, which probably represents a somewhat quixotic and unpredictable source of tension on her unconscious mind. She also has the familiar high order grand elevations of the Sun and Mercury. In addition, she has a very active chart with an extremely high GPI of 44 and a staggering P/N of +3.89—one of the highest positive P/Ns I have ever seen.

This chart shows evidence of an extraordinarily high number of positive forces at work. She has six high order positive grand elevations: Sun, Venus, Mercury, Jupiter, Uranus, and Pluto. There are five planets located in the Hidek position, while Mercury is located in the Exdek position. There is also a very rare band elevation located above the twenty-one degree position. If that is not enough, she also has a binary eclipse involving the Sun, Mercury, and Venus.

This constellation of forces probably helped allow her to remain somewhat functional despite her illness. However, we once again see the familiar pattern of high-order stimulation of the Sun, Mercury, and Pluto. The overstimulation of the planets that represent integral parts of the psyche is a recurrent theme in the astrological presentation of schizophrenia.

The temporal environment represented by the birth chart displayed here is extremely positive (+17,116). This may indicate a propitious time for a birth, with the caveat that there may be some intrinsic imbalance within the psychic forces. The imbalance, however, is more than compensated for by the presence of a

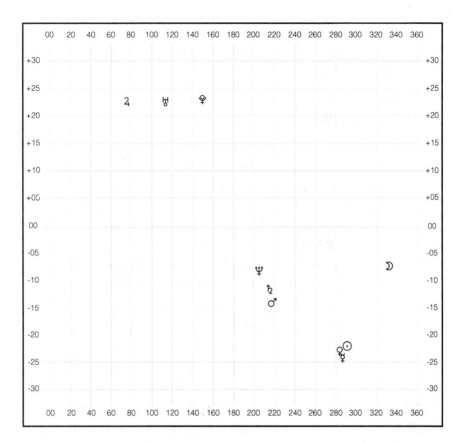

Chart 14: Frances

large number of planets located in the Hidek position. Indeed, in this chart, the band elevation probably exerts a positive influence on the native as most of the planets within the band are located in the Hidek position. Again we see an example of the mitigation of an otherwise negative condition by the presence of a high positive temporal environment.

Marker Aspects for Schizophrenia (14)

Conjunction: Mercury/Venus

Sextile: Venus/Mars

Square: Uranus/Neptune

Trine: Moon/Saturn

Parallels: Jupiter/Uranus, Neptune/Moon, Sun/Venus, Mercury/ Venus

Contraparallel: Sun/Mercury

Hidek: Sun, Pluto

Proximity elevation: Jupiter/Uranus parallel

Grand elevations:
  1) Sun (Sun/Mercury conjunction, Sun/Venus conjunction, Sun/ Venus parallel, Contraparallels [Sun/Jupiter, Sun/Uranus, Sun/Pluto, Sun/Mercury], Band elevation [Sun-Mercury-Venus-Jupiter-Pluto-Uranus], Hidek Sun, Proximity elevations [Sun/Jupiter and Sun/Pluto contraparallels]
  2) Mercury (Mercury/Venus conjunction, Sun/Mercury conjunction, Mercury/Venus parallel, Contraparallels [Mercury/Jupiter, Mercury/Uranus, Sun/Mercury, Mercury/Pluto] Band elevation [Sun-Mercury Venus-Jupiter-Pluto-Uranus])

The GPI of Frances' chart is 44 and the P/N is +3.89.

CARL

Carl was given the diagnosis of paranoid schizophrenia when he was nineteen. He was hospitalized once when he insisted on playing religious music very loudly for days at a time. He had also refused to bathe, put on clean clothes, or leave his room for three weeks. He told his family that he was receiving energy from the sky that helped him communicate with nature in a way they could not understand. He has been unable to hold down a job but he is able to take classes at a local trade school. As long as he takes his medication, Carl is able to attend classes and carry out a normal life. Each time he forgets his medication or stops it voluntarily, the behaviors return and his family ushers him back into treatment.

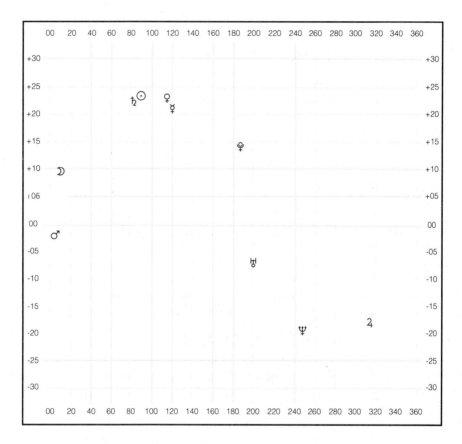

Chart 15: Carl

Carl's birth chart shows nine marker aspects for schizophrenia. Again we see multiple elevations involving the Sun, Mercury, and Pluto as well as a Hidek placement for the Sun. Three elevations involving Mars and three involving Jupiter give him an above-average planetary index for both these planets. A very low negative P/N (-0.273) combined with a healthy GPI of 28 indicates that Carl might experience a downward drift as he ages. His grand elevation of the Sun is negative. This fact probably adds to the negative psychic pressure which fuels the process of schizophrenia.

Marker Aspects for Schizophrenia (9)
Conjunction: Mercury/Venus

Trine: Neptune/Mars

Squares: Sun/Mars, Venus/Uranus

Opposition: Pluto/Mars

Parallels: Sun/Venus, Venus/Mercury

Hidek: Sun

Grand elevation:
>   Sun (Sun/Saturn conjunction, Sun/Mars square, Sun/Pluto square, Sun/Venus parallel, Sun/Saturn parallel, Triangle elevation [Sun-Saturn-Venus, Hidek Sun])

The GPI for Carl's chart is 28and the P/N is -0.273.

High Risk Transits for Schizophrenia

When the following conditions involving transiting planets occur, persons who exhibit signs of Schizophrenia can experience an intensification of symptoms.

- Neptune/Mars trine
- Saturn/Moon trine
- Hidek Sun
- Jupiter/Uranus parallel
- Venus/Mercury parallel
- Neptune/Moon parallel

9 Attention Deficit Hyperactivity Disorder

ATTENTION DEFICIT HYPERACTIVITY DISORDER (ADHD) IS THE MOST common disruptive behavior disorder in children. It affects 3 to 5% of all children, and the male-female ratio is 5–10: 1. ADHD is thought to coexist with conduct disorders or oppositional defiant disorder. It also occurs with specific developmental disorders, and has been associated with specific learning disorders in some children.

The exact cause of ADHD is unknown. It is believed to reflect the existence of subtle neurological impairments that may be associated with perinatal trauma and early malnutrition. ADHD is certainly a familial disorder, and is likely to have a genetic component. Children who have parents with the disorder are at high risk for the development of the disorder.

Perinatal complications may also play a causative role in its development. ADHD children have a higher incidence of antepartum hemorrhage, prolonged maternal labor, low Apgar scores at one minute, and are likely to have soft neurological signs of minimal brain dysfunction. A high percentage of children affected with septic meningitis also develop indications of ADHD.

Twenty to twenty-five percent of children with ADHD continue to show symptoms into adolescence and adulthood. There is a tendency to develop a coexistent conduct disorder, become delinquent, or develop an antisocial personality disorder. A significant number of adults who seek treatment for cocaine abuse have histories of childhood ADHD.

In order to qualify for the diagnosis of ADHD, a child must begin to display symptoms before the age of seven and have shown at least six months of persistent pathology. The most common symptoms of ADHD are inattention, hyperactivity, and impulsivity. These symptoms may manifest as six or more of the following:

- Frequent fidgeting with hands or feet or squirming; adolescents may report feelings of restlessness
- Difficulty remaining seated when required
- Easy distractibility by extraneous stimuli
- Difficulty awaiting turns in games or groups
- Blurting out answers before questions have been completed
- Difficulty following through on instructions from others
- Difficulty sustaining attention in tasks or play activities
- Shifting from one uncompleted activity to another
- Difficulty playing quietly
- Talking excessively
- Interrupting others or intruding on others
- Lack of attention to what is being said
- Frequent loss of things necessary for tasks or activities at school or at home
- Frequent engagement in physically dangerous activities without considering possible consequences *

Numerous research studies show that children who meet DSM-IV criteria for the diagnosis of ADHD show a 75% reduction in their symptoms, develop improved self-esteem, and develop improved rapport with parents and teachers when they are given psychostimulants.

STUDY 4: ADHD

In this study, the birth charts of sixteen children with a two-year history of treatment for ADHD were examined. The results of the analysis for these patients, as compared to the results obtained from the analysis of the control charts, are shown here.

* Reprinted with permission from the Diagnostic and Statistical Manual of Mental Disorders, Fourth Edition. Copyright 1994 American Psychiatric Association.

Planetary Indices	Test	Control	(Change)
Sun	+215	+181	+16%
Moon	-95	+112	-117%
Mercury	+128	+170	-25%
Venus	+197	+133	+34%
Mars	-353	-450	+22%
Jupiter	+119	+194	-39%
Saturn	-813	-604	-26%
Uranus	-78	+137	-175%
Neptune	+113	+148	-24%
Pluto	+145	+112	+23%

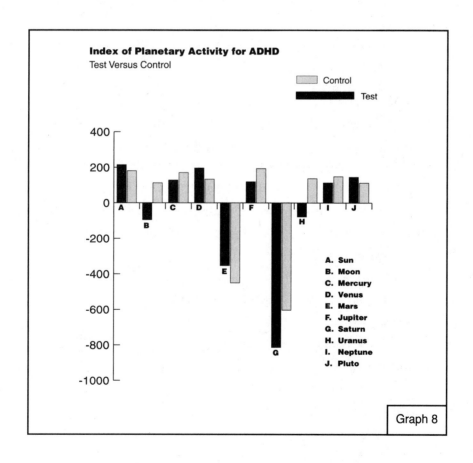

Specific Planetary Markers for ADHD (39)

Conjunctions:
  Saturn/Mars, Saturn/Neptune, Saturn/Uranus

Sextiles:
  Jupiter/Moon, Sun/Neptune, Uranus/Mercury,
  Jupiter/Mars, Sun/Saturn, Mercury/Mars

Squares:
  Pluto/Venus, Neptune/Mars, Venus/Mars

Trines:
  Sun/Pluto

Oppositions:
  Jupiter/Saturn, Jupiter/Neptune

Parallels:
  Uranus/Neptune, Saturn/Uranus, Saturn/Neptune,
  Sun/Mercury, Sun/Venus

Contraparallels:
  Jupiter/Neptune, Jupiter/Saturn, Jupiter/Uranus,
  Jupiter/Sun, Sun/Neptune, Moon/Venus

Triangle elevation:
  Saturn-Neptune-Uranus

Hidek:
  Neptune, Saturn, Jupiter, Uranus

Exdek:
  Uranus, Moon

Proximity elevations:
  Saturn/Neptune, Neptune/Uranus

Eclipses:
  Saturn/Mars

Binary eclipse:
  Saturn/Neptune/Uranus

Grand elevations:
  Neptune, Uranus

The GPI for this group is 34.69 and the P/N is -0.833.

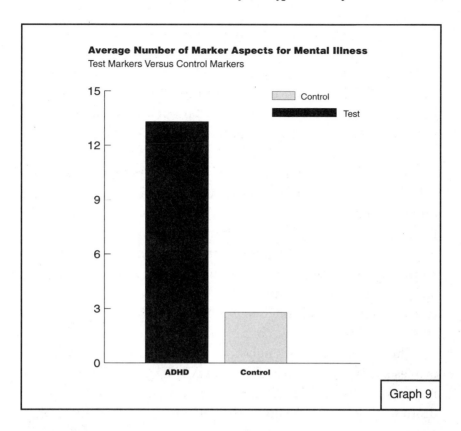

Average Number of Marker Aspects for Mental Illness
Test Markers Versus Control Markers

Graph 9

SATURN, URANUS, AND ADHD

Before we begin our analysis of specific test charts that display the above characteristics, I would like to point out some of the more remarkable attributes of the data. The ADHD test patients possessed the most unique and unusual birth charts of all the groups tested. They had the highest GPI (34.69), the lowest P/N (-0.833), the highest number of Saturn eclipses (12), the highest number of binary eclipses (4), and the highest average number of marker aspects per test chart (13.31). These charts also demonstrated the highest net change from baseline for the planets Uranus (-175%) and Saturn (-26%), as well as a large increase in negative Moon activity (-117%). High order negative Saturn indices and a high probability of negative grand elevations for Neptune and Uranus also rank among the most remarkable characteristics of these test charts.

In the birth chart, Saturn represents our limitations and boundaries. Modern science has verified through the use of a series of planetary probes the Saturn has the most complex set of rings in existence. The force field of these rings may be responsible for Saturn's gravitational field. Gravity, constriction, compression, and rule-setting are all functions of Saturn.

In ADHD, Saturn displays some very unusual patterns of behavior. ADHD is characterized by a disease process which compels the patient to test limits within structured settings, engage in often unpredictable and sometimes dangerous physical activities, become easily distractible, and shift from one uncompleted activity to another. The observation that ADHD patients also demonstrate massive changes in their Saturn profiles that may be correlated with extreme limit-testing behaviors is a potentially revolutionary breakthrough in our understanding of how celestial events may impact human behavior.

The association of high-order Saturn elevations with an increased risk for the development of ADHD is another potentially important observation. Saturn is associated with hardship and death in all its forms. Many of the patients in this study have high-order negative Saturn elevations and a history of birth trauma.

Planetary eclipses are fairly common celestial occurrences, but binary eclipses, which occur when three planets are in conjunction and parallel to each other simultaneously, are rare and signify exponential releases of planetary energy. This particular group of patients exhibited four binary eclipses (more than all the other test charts combined) involving Saturn, as well as a Saturn/Mars eclipse. This is a massive and extraordinary release of Saturn energy.

But perhaps even more extraordinary is the fact that this shift in Saturn potential is coupled with an even larger change in Uranus potential in the same test group.

Uranus circles the Sun on its belly at a 90° angle to the ecliptic, unlike any other planet in the solar system. Astrologically, it represents the rebellious, unpredictable, and highly inventive aspects of the human psyche.

The archetypal correlation of Uranus with rebels and unpredictable behavior is also well grounded. Uranus is associated with the rebellious Titan Prometheus who defied the will of Zeus in order to help humankind. Once, he tricked Zeus into choosing the fat and bones of the sacrificial bull while leaving the choice meat for humanity. Angered, Zeus withheld the gift of fire so men and women would have to eat their meat raw. Again, Prometheus defied Zeus, stealing sparks of divine fire from Olympus and giving them to humankind—an act for which he paid dearly.

Remarkably, in this most unpredictable and rebellious group of all the patients tested, I observed the largest and most significant change in the activity of the planet Uranus that I have ever measured. The activity shift was indicative of an increase in the negative energy potential for this planet. The negative attributes of Uranus are exactly the same as the major characteristics of the illness of ADHD—rebelliousness, unpredictability, and defiance. No other single group in this research study demonstrated this high a level of associativeness with one particular planetary energy source.

In all of the binary eclipses and most of the planetary eclipses, both Saturn and Uranus are involved. When the massive release of Saturn energy and the tremendous increase of negative Uranian potential are examined in light of the presenting symptoms of the ADHD test group, one cannot easily dismiss the association.

Furthermore, there has been a large increase in the number of newly diagnosed cases of ADHD over the last ten years. Has the high declination Uranus/Neptune parallel of the last few years combined with a high degree of interactivity with the planet Saturn served to influence the development of this shift? What changes for society are presaged by the birth of such a large number of rebellious, unpredictable adults?

Now, let's examine four birth charts from the test group that display a large number of marker aspects for ADHD. All names used to identify the patients are pseudonyms.

TAYLOR

Given up for adoption when he was three months old, Taylor always felt that he was different from the other kids in his classroom. He could never just sit in his chair and wait for his teachers to call on him. He liked to walk around the classroom and talk to his friends, even when asked to sit down. On several occasions he was sent to the principal's office for punishment and redirection. He fights with his brothers and sisters and seems unable to take care of his possessions. He cannot sit still long enough to watch television or to play with friends in a quiet manner. His grades at school are poor.

Taylor was started on a psychostimulant by his doctor, and within a few weeks his behavior and interactions at home and at

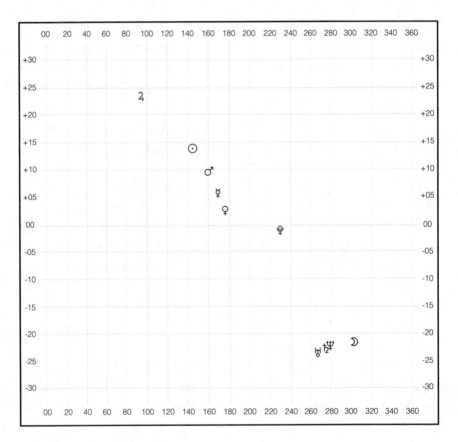

Chart 16: Taylor

school improved. His parents are happy about this, but they are concerned that he may need to be on medication for the rest of his life.

Taylor's birth chart displays a large number of important aspects of ADHD. The GPI is very high and the P/N is exceptionally low. He has a high-order negative Saturn index, a high-order negative grand elevation of Uranus, and a binary eclipse of Saturn. In addition, he has a plenary elevation located in the area of high declination. The activity of Uranus in this chart may also be rendered more erratic by its elevation by extreme declination.

Saturn/Neptune parallels are associated with an increased risk for physical injury and death. When combined with declinational aspects to Pluto, the Saturn/Neptune parallel can presage a greatly increased risk for premature death from all causes. One of the risk factors associated with the development of ADHD is perinatal trauma and injury. Taylor experienced birth trauma secondary to an antepartum hemorrhage which his mother suffered. He required treatment in the ICU for several days prior to being released.

Markers for ADHD (17)

Conjunctions:
    Saturn/Neptune, Saturn/Uranus

Sextile:
    Mars/Jupiter

Parallels:
    Saturn/Neptune, Saturn/Uranus, Neptune/Uranus

Contraparallels:
    Jupiter/Neptune, Jupiter/Saturn, Jupiter/Uranus

Hidek:
    Jupiter, Saturn, Neptune

Exdek:
    Uranus

Proximity elevations:
    Saturn/Neptune

Binary eclipse:
    Saturn/Uranus/Neptune

Grand elevations:

1) Uranus (Saturn/Uranus conjunction, Uranus/Mars trine, Venus/Uranus square, Jupiter/Uranus opposition, Longitudinal proximity elevation [Uranus/Neptune, Saturn/Uranus parallel, Neptune/Uranus parallel, Jupiter/Uranus contraparallel, Plenary elevation [Jupiter-Neptune-Saturn-Uranus-Moon], Exdek Uranus, Binary eclipse [Saturn-Uranus-Neptune])

2) Neptune (Saturn/Neptune conjunction, Neptune/Mars trine, Jupiter/Neptune opposition, Saturn/Neptune parallel, Neptune/Uranus parallel, Neptune/Moon parallel, Jupiter/ Neptune contraparallel, Plenary elevation [Jupiter-Neptune Saturn-Uranus-Moon], Hidek Neptune, Proximity elevation [Saturn/Neptune parallel], Binary eclipse [Saturn-Uranus-Neptune])

The GPI for Taylor's chart is 37 and the P/N is -0.233.

SANDY

Sandy has been in treatment for ADHD for two years. Before going into treatment, she had been in three different day care centers and was expelled from all of them. She has gotten into fights with the other clients, and she often runs into the street in an attempt to get away from staff when they try to redirect her. She takes special classes at school because she has difficulty sitting still and argues with her teachers. She has set several fires at home and she has been caught shoplifting at several shops in her neighborhood. Sandy's birth chart shows eighteen signs consistent with ADHD.

Her chart displays one of the lowest P/Ns I have ever measured (-0.146). She is too young to have experienced much in life, but when one considers her extremely high GPI (41) with the eight negative grand elevations in her chart, there is substantial reason to worry. Her Saturn index is particularly high, with fourteen negative

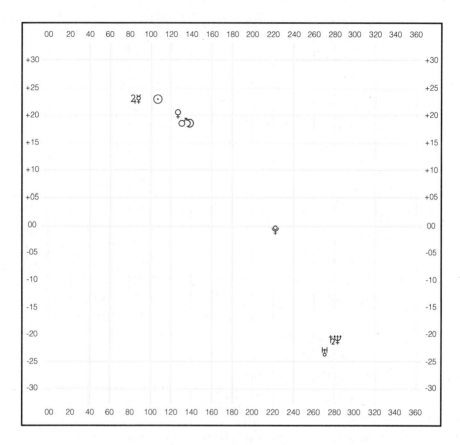

Chart 17: Sandy

Saturn elevations in her chart. Note that she also has a high declination band elevation, two planetary eclipses, and a binary eclipse. This is an excellent example of an astrological birth chart with a very high complexity index. The complexity index is calculated by computing the sum of the triangle elevations, quad elevations, plenary elevations, band elevations, planetary eclipses, and proximity elevations. The resulting value may be positive or negative. A high positive index is considered to be beneficial, while a high negative complexity index is extremely deleterious.

Marker Aspects for ADHD (18)

Conjunction: Saturn/Neptune

Trine: Sun/Pluto

Square: Venus/Pluto

Parallels: Sun/Mercury, Saturn/Uranus, Uranus/Neptune, Saturn/Neptune

Contraparallels: Jupiter/Uranus, Jupiter/Saturn Jupiter/Neptune, Sun/Neptune

Hidek: Jupiter, Saturn, Neptune

Exdek: Uranus

Proximity elevation: Saturn/Neptune parallel

Grand elevations:
   1) Uranus (Mercury/Uranus opposition, Saturn/Uranus longitudinal proximity elevation, Saturn/Uranus parallel, Uranus/Neptune parallel, Jupiter/Uranus contraparallel, Mercury/Uranus contraparallel, Sun/ Uranus contraparallel, Band elevation [Sun-Neptune-Saturn-Uranus-Jupiter-Mercury], Exdek Uranus)

   2) Neptune (Saturn/Neptune conjunction, Sun/Neptune opposition, Uranus/Neptune parallel, Saturn/Neptune parallel, Jupiter/Neptune contraparallel, Mercury/Neptune contraparallel, Sun/Neptune contraparallel, Hidek Neptune, Proximity elevation [Saturn/Neptune parallel])

The GPI for Sandy's chart is 41 and the P/N is -0.146.

SUSAN

Susan's chart displays a number of familiar aspects that have been associated with ADHD. She has taken psychostimulant medication for six years. When she forgets to take it, her behavior regresses within days. She seldom finishes chores given to her by her parents, talks excessively in class, interrupts others often, has difficulty playing quietly, fidgets and squirms a lot, seldom completes a game or task before demanding to start another, and has extreme difficulty remaining seated in class.

Susan experienced severe perinatal trauma. Her mother fell down a flight of stairs when she was eight months pregnant and almost delivered prematurely. She then remained in the hospital for the remainder of the pregnancy because she developed septic meningitis. Susan was born two weeks early and required a three-week stay in the ICU before going home.

By the time she was four years old, it was noticeable that Susan had difficulty following instructions. She became progressively more difficult to handle as she got older, and eventually her parents sought psychiatric help for guidance in managing her behavior.

Susan's birth chart displays eleven negative Saturn elevations, a Saturn-Neptune-Uranus binary eclipse, and seven negative Neptune elevations. She also has an Exdek Uranus.

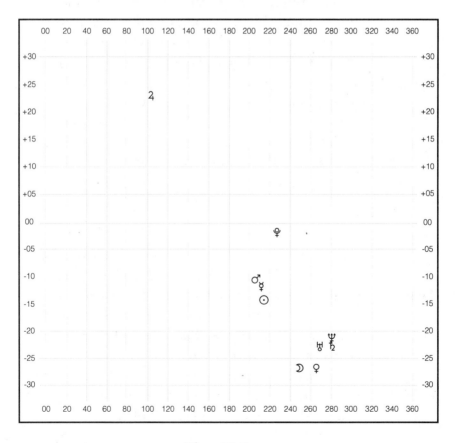

Chart 18: Susan

Marker aspects for ADHD (19)

Conjunctions: Saturn/Neptune, Saturn/Uranus

Sextiles: Sun/Saturn, Mercury/Uranus, Sun/Neptune

Parallels: Saturn/Neptune, Saturn/Uranus, Uranus/Neptune

Contraparallels: Jupiter/Saturn, Jupiter/Neptune, Jupiter/Uranus

Hidek: Jupiter, Saturn, Neptune

Exdek: Moon, Uranus

Binary eclipse: Saturn/Neptune/Uranus

Grand elevations:

1) Uranus (Saturn/Uranus conjunction, Mars/Uranus sextile, Saturn/Uranus parallel, Uranus/Neptune parallel, Jupiter/ Uranus contraparallel, quad elevation [Jupiter-Saturn-Neptune-Uranus], Exdek Uranus, Binary eclipse [Saturn-Neptune Uranus])

2) Neptune (Saturn/Neptune conjunction, Saturn/Neptune parallel, Uranus/Neptune parallel, Jupiter/Neptune contraparallel, Quad elevation (Jupiter-Saturn-Neptune-Uranus], Hidek Neptune, Binary eclipse [Saturn-Neptune-Uranus])

The GPI of Susan's chart is 35 and the P/N is -0.52.

WILLIAM

William's chart has nineteen marker aspects associated with ADHD. He also has one of the highest number of elevations that I have ever seen in one chart (50). His chart has seven proximity elevations, two quads, two binary eclipses, and eight grand elevations. Fortunately, he has a balance of positive and negative grand elevations. He has a high-order negative Saturn index (13) combined with a high-order negative Neptune index (11) and a high-order negative Uranus index. This triad of intense negative energy is a common presentation in the birth charts of ADHD patients.

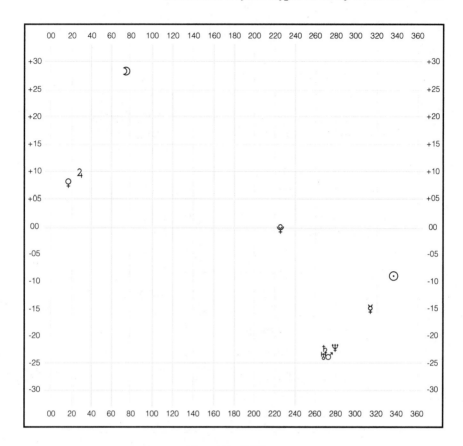

Chart 19: William

Marker Aspects for ADHD (19)

Conjunctions: Saturn/Neptune, Saturn/Uranus

Sextiles: Moon/Jupiter

Squares: Neptune/Mars

Parallels: Sun/Mercury, Saturn/Uranus, Saturn/Neptune, Uranus/Neptune

Contraparallels: Jupiter/Saturn, Jupiter/Uranus, Jupiter/Neptune

Triangle elevation: Saturn-Neptune-Uranus

Hidek: Jupiter, Saturn, Uranus, Neptune

Binary eclipse: Saturn-Neptune-Uranus

Grand elevations:

1) Uranus: Saturn/Uranus conjunction, Mercury/Uranus square, Sun/Uranus square, Mars/Uranus square, Uranus/Neptune parallel, Jupiter/Uranus contraparallel, triangle elevation [Saturn-Neptune-Uranus], Quad elevation [Jupiter-Saturn- Uranus-Neptune], Hidek Uranus, Binary eclipse [Saturn- Neptune-Uranus])

2) (Neptune: Saturn/Neptune conjunction, Mars/Neptune square, Sun/Neptune square, Jupiter/Neptune opposition, Uranus/Neptune parallel, Jupiter/Neptune contraparallel, Saturn/Neptune/Uranus triangle elevation, quad elevation: Jupiter/Saturn/Uranus/Neptune, Hidek Neptune, proximity elevation: Jupiter/Neptune contraparallel, binary eclipse: Saturn/Neptune/Uranus)

The GPI for William's chart is 50 and the P/N is -0.7.

High Risk Transits for ADHD

When the following conditions involving transiting planets occur, persons who exhibit signs of ADHD can experience an intensification of symptoms.

- Sun/Pluto trine
- Saturn/Mars parallel
- Uranus/Neptune parallel
- Pluto/Venus square
- Saturn/Mars conjunction
- Exdek Uranus
- Jupiter/Mars sextile

10   Addictive Disorders

ADDICTIVE DISORDERS ARE AMONG THE OLDEST MENTAL HEALTH problems known, and they continue to plague us today. A recent edition of *Time* magazine (May 1997, pp. 69–76) featured a story that chronicled modern research and epidemiological surveys of addictive disorder in the United States. According to the article, during the month prior to publication 200,000 people used heroin, 800,000 people used amphetamines, 10 million people used marijuana, and 11 million people abused alcohol in the United States.

Addictions are among the most costly and problematic conditions facing the modern world. Wars have been fought over the drug problem. Major international treaties and two permanent international bodies exist that are aimed at controlling the tide of drug trafficking. In the U.S. alone billions of dollars are spent every year on the purchase of drugs and in the treatment of addictive disorders.

The terminology used to describe addictive disorders has changed significantly over the years. Public perceptions of what is and what is not an addiction have also changed dramatically. Many people now propose that almost anything can become an addiction. This includes (but is not limited to) relationships, television, chocolate, food, sex, shopping, movies, exercise, and computers. Indeed, almost any arena of human interaction has become suspect of harboring addictive potential.

Scientists have adopted more strict criteria for the diagnosis of addictive disorder/psychoactive substance dependence, including:

- Persistent desire or one or more unsuccessful efforts to control the substance or behavior

- Frequent intoxication
- Diminished effect with continued use
- Continued use despite knowledge of harmful effects
- Withdrawal symptoms
- Using the substance or behavior to avoid withdrawal symptoms
- Symptoms persisting for more than one month*

Alcoholism (alcohol dependence) affects millions of Americans. A majority (70%) of Americans drink alcohol on occasion. About 12% (20% of men and 9% of women) are defined as heavy drinkers who drink almost every day and become intoxicated several times a month. In the United States, 10% of the drinking population consumes 50% of all alcohol. Alcohol dependence runs in families, and children of alcoholics are at high risk for developing the disorder. Alcohol is very addictive and, when used in excess, can cause serious health problems including liver damage, brain damage, delirium, hallucinations, amnesia, and dementia.

Amphetamines are extremely addictive and very dangerous. They are most commonly abused by students, long-distance truck drivers, and teenagers. Clinically, amphetamines are used as appetite suppressants. Amphetamines cause a massive release of dopamine within the brain, and drugs that inhibit this release also block the amphetamine "high."

Cocaine is a highly addictive psychoactive substance that has been in use for centuries. It is refined from substances in the coca plant and it is usually smoked, snorted, or injected. Cocaine has a rapid onset and blocks the normal absorption of dopamine into the brain. It has been associated with seizures, delusional disorders, and sudden death through heart problems.

Opiate addiction is one of the oldest addictions known to humankind. There are currently an estimated 600,000 opiate addicts in the United States. Opiate derivatives include heroin, codeine, methadone, morphine, opium, and meperidine. Opiates

* Reprinted with permission from the Diagnostic and Statistical Manual of Mental Disorders, Fourth Edition. Copyright 1994 American Psychiatric Association.

are usually smoked, injected, inhaled, or taken orally. They also cause a massive release of dopamine into the brain. A major problem with opiate abuse is overdose.

STUDY 5: ADDICTIVE DISORDERS

This study was designed to determine the presence of astrological markers for alcoholism, amphetamine dependence, and cocaine addiction in the birth charts of thirteen patients. All patients included in this study have been in treatment for their addictions for periods ranging from one year to fifteen years. The data for these charts are listed below.

Planetary Indices	Test Group	Control Group	(Change)
Sun	+182	+181	+0.55%
Moon	-73	+112	-153%
Mercury	-76	+170	-224%
Venus	+111	+133	-16.5%
Mars	-121	-450	+372%
Jupiter	+216	+194	+10.2%
Saturn	-608	-604	-1.0%
Uranus	+150	+137	+8.7%
Neptune	+205	+148	+27.8%
Pluto	+134	+112	+16.4%

Specific Planetary Markers for Addictive Disorder (26)

Conjunctions:
  Jupiter/Pluto, Jupiter/Uranus

Trines:
  Moon/Pluto, Uranus/Neptune, Sun/Uranus, Saturn/Pluto

Sextiles:
  Sun/Jupiter, Jupiter/Neptune, Uranus/Mars

Squares:
  Venus/Saturn, Sun/Neptune, Sun/Mars

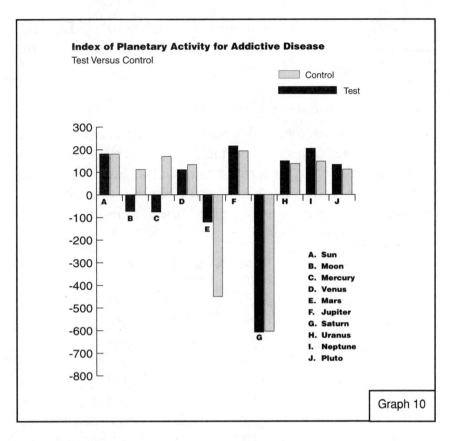

Index of Planetary Activity for Addictive Disease
Test Versus Control

A. Sun
B. Moon
C. Mercury
D. Venus
E. Mars
F. Jupiter
G. Saturn
H. Uranus
I. Neptune
J. Pluto

Graph 10

Oppositions:
Jupiter/Mars, Moon/Venus, Moon/Uranus, Moon/Neptune

Parallels:
Jupiter/Uranus, Saturn/Mercury

Contraparallels:
Moon/Mercury, Saturn/Mars

Hidek:
Pluto, Mercury

Exdek:
Moon, Mars

Grand elevation:
Pluto

Eclipses:
Any planetary eclipse involving Jupiter
The GPI for the test group is 28.69 and the P/N is -0.837

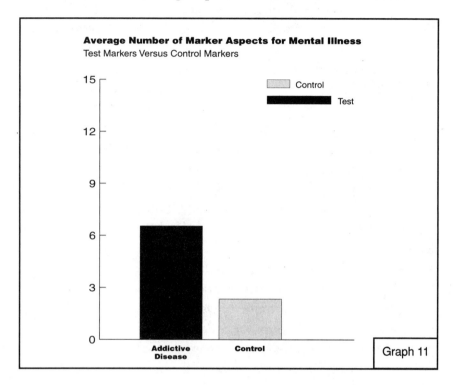

Average Number of Marker Aspects for Mental Illness
Test Markers Versus Control Markers

Graph 11

This data represents a surprising and exciting discovery: the Mercury planetary index dropped 224% and the Mars index rose 372%. The shifts of planetary activity in this test group suggest that the primary forces that impel the addictive drive are the conflicting Mars and Mercury archetypes.

Mercury is associated with rational thought, the mind, perception, and mental energy. A drop in the Mercury index indicates an increase in the number of negative elevations involving this planet. Compared to the control group, Mercury tends to exhibit an enormous increase in negative behavior—inconsistency, lacking a sense of purpose, and mental strain or stagnation. Distorted perceptions are the hallmarks of negative Mercury activity.

Many addicts recognize that an integral part of the addictive process is the concept of "stinking thinking," a slang term used to describe the cognitive distortions that often surround the thought patterns associated with drug or substance craving. These distortions cause the addict to become consumed with thoughts about the drug or substance until it can be acquired. These thoughts often take devious and destructive turns, and hundreds of thousands of addicts have been incarcerated for (or killed while) committing crimes in order to feed their habits—a fact that is not often a deterrent when the craving becomes acute. One could scarcely imagine a process more definitive of negative Mercury activity.

An increase in the Mars index signals an increase in the number of positive elevations involving this planet. This is associated with an increase in positive Martian attributes—strong impulsive nature, energy, increased sex drive, and enhanced creative ability. Mars is the planet that is most strongly associated with aggression, energy, and the baser instincts which impel human emotion. When a strong Martian impulse strikes, nothing can dispel it.

The Mars force is a major power to be dealt with when it is activated. In this test group, the index of activity observed for the planet Mars indicates that, as a group, their Martian energies are greatly enhanced. When one combines the huge increase in positive Mars energy with the large increase in negative Mercury energy, the addictive process may become inadvertently empowered. This takes place because the normally cogent and rational forces of Mercury are critical allies in the process of controlling strong Martian impulses when they arise. If one then combines enhanced Martian forces with weakened or ineffective Mercury defenses within the same psyche, the perfect psychic environment for the growth and sustenance of an addictive life pattern is created.

A deeper analysis of this combination of energies may yield a more thorough understanding of the archetypal forces that impel the addictive process. The creative urges that are propelled explosively into the conscious mind by the unstoppable Mars drive are the cornerstone around which the addictive cycle is sculpted within the psyche. The Martian craving process is central to sustaining the addictive cycle. The more the craving increases, the more the usage increases, and the more the usage increases, the more it takes to satisfy the craving. Thus, the cycle ensues, and unless treatment is given the addict becomes ensnared in a web of destructive thoughts and behaviors. The absence of the counterbalance of a strong positive Mercury combined with the additional impelling force of increased Jupiter activity serve to sustain and nourish the seeds of the addictive process.

Greatly exaggerated Jupiter forces are also a major aspect of the astrological profile of this group. Jupiter is astrologically associated with expansion and excess. Jupiter eclipses are associated with a tremendous increase in power, acquisitiveness, charisma, and the ability to influence others to one's way of thinking. Six out of thirteen members of the addictive disorders test group displayed planetary eclipses involving Jupiter in their birth charts, while only two out of twenty-four members of the control group had such eclipses. This tremendous increase in the number of Jupiter eclipses in the test group may provide impetus for the sometimes ravenous excesses seen in the life patterns of addicts.

People who are addicted to drugs or alcohol have been known to squander entire fortunes in service to their cravings. The names of singers, movie stars, world leaders, politicians, and professionals from every walk of life who have lost their careers because of drug or alcohol habits reads like a list from *Who's Who*. The power of the Jupiter eclipse is staggering, and we will examine some further associations with this uncommon celestial event in a later chapter.

Now we will examine several test charts that display a large number of marker aspects for the addictive disorders.

CAMERON

Cameron has been a cocaine addict for six years. He first snorted coke at a college party. Soon after, he became a regular at his friend's home, mostly because he could get free drugs if he brought a girl with him. He liked the rush and the feeling of calm and peace that he got every time he used the stuff, although it seemed that it took more and more every time.

At first, Cameron never let the drugs interfere with school, work, or his relationships. Then his friend moved away, and he needed a new source. Finding one wasn't an easy job, but propelled by need, he did. His bubble burst when the new dealer turned out to be a cop.

Cameron was arrested for possession of cocaine and served nine months in jail, losing his scholarship and his job. When he got out, his habit only got worse—his craving had not diminished at all. His family checked him into two different drug treatment centers, but he did not complete the programs at either one. Today, Cameron spends his disability checks on feeding his habit.

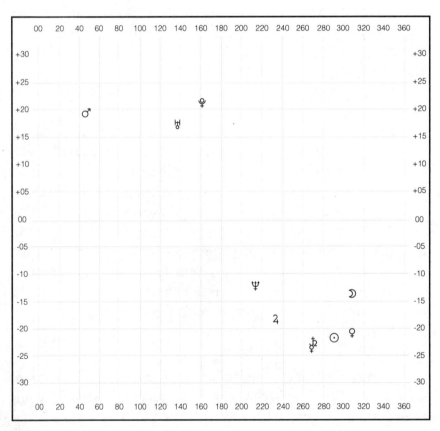

Chart 20: Cameron

Cameron's birth chart gives us useful insight into the possible astrological origins of his habit. He has a negative grand elevation of Mercury and Pluto. The focus of energy in his chart points to an intense acceleration of negative cognitive force and a massive release of deep unconscious mind activity. Pluto's energy is associated with a higher order form of Martian energy and therefore the two forces are related in their capacity for intense, unrelenting change when activated. Cameron cannot control his craving for cocaine no matter how hard he tries.

His cognitive abilities are further inhibited by a Hidek Saturn/Mercury eclipse, which forms part of a plenary elevation that also involves Pluto and the Sun. One interpretation of this configuration is that Cameron's inner drive is potentiated by the Pluto and Mercury grand elevations, but the forces driving this change do not allow for adequate mental or physical control of the energies. A somewhat lower than normal P/N probably adds to his illness.

Marker Aspects for Addictive Disorder (8)

Trines:
   Saturn/Pluto

Sextiles:
   Sun/Jupiter

Oppositions:
   Mars/Jupiter, Moon/Uranus

Parallels:
   Mercury/Saturn

Hidek:
   Mercury, Pluto

Grand elevation:
   Pluto (Saturn/Pluto trine, Contraparallels
   [Pluto/Mars, Sun/Pluto, Saturn/Pluto, Mercury/Pluto],
   Plenary elevation [Sun-Mercury-Venus-Saturn-Pluto],
   Hidek Pluto)

The GPI for Cameron's chart is 33 and the P/N is -0.50.

GEORGE

George is a recovering alcoholic. At one time in his life he drank up to one quart of vodka per day. He has been hospitalized four times for medical problems associated with drinking. He also has six DUI convictions and his license has been suspended twice. He has been married three times and has lost custody of his children because of behavior problems that arise when he drinks. George feels that without Alcoholics Anonymous and the support of his sponsor, he would surely be dead.

Most of George's marker aspects for addictive disease are related to Jupiter. Jupiter is associated with courts, lawyers, excesses, gluttony, and wealth. George has experienced a great

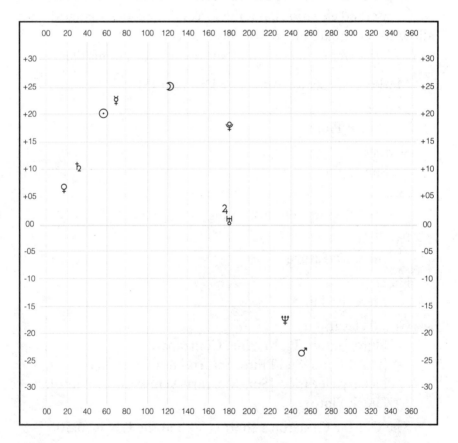

Chart 21: George

deal of each of the above. Unfortunately, as a result of his illness, he has lost his money, his family, and his health. The Jupiter/Uranus eclipse is a strong predictor for addictive potential.

When Mars is elevated by extreme declination, its energies are rendered more erratic and, in many cases, more extreme. In the case of addictions, an Exdek Mars adds force to the energies impelling the craving and cognitive distortions. In this chart, Mars has an index of -200, which is less than half the value for the control group (-450). This indicates that George also has a positive elevation of his Mars forces relative to the control group. Increased Mars energy combined with the expansive forces of Jupiter may have served to create a nearly-insurmountable addictive urge in this patient.

Marker Aspects for Addictive Disorder (9)

Conjunctions:
  Jupiter/Pluto, Jupiter/Uranus

Sextile:
  Jupiter/Neptune

Parallel:
  Jupiter/Uranus

Hidek:
  Mercury

Exdek:
  Moon, Mars

Eclipse:
  Jupiter/Uranus

Grand elevation:
  Pluto (Sun/Pluto trine, Neptune/Pluto sextile, Moon/Pluto sextile, Longitudinal proximity elevation [Pluto/Uranus-Pluto/Neptune contraparallel], Proximity elevation [Pluto/Neptune contraparallel])

The GPI for George's chart is 27 and the P/N is +2.86.

HARRY

Harry tried amphetamines for the first time when he was sixteen years old. The rush was exciting and invigorating beyond all of his wildest dreams. He was hooked immediately. His use was confined primarily to parties and weekends during his college years, but when he took his first job after college, he began to succumb more and more deeply to his cravings.

Harry landed a prestigious job with a large architectural firm and he found that he could work longer when he used speed. Eventually, his hours at work began to stretch into days, and he noticed that his appetite for food was nearly nonexistent.

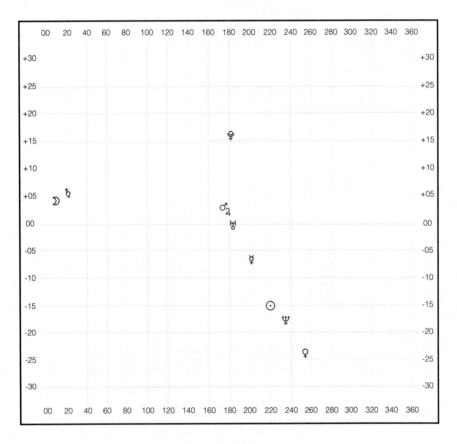

Chart 22: Harry

He survived this way for two years before anyone noticed. Then one day at work, his supervisor remarked that Harry's speech seemed a little rapid. Harry had been worrying that he was using too much of the stuff and now that his boss had possibly noticed his habit, he was unable to contain his anxiety. He panicked and ran out of the room shouting that he felt a little weak and needed to go to the bathroom.

He was asked to take a random urine drug screen. The test was positive for methamphetamine, and Harry was asked to seek treatment for drug abuse. During his evaluation, he admitted that he had not slept normally for more than a year. His drug habit cost him more than $2,000 a month.

In Harry's chart we see that five out of seven of his marker aspects for addictive disorders involve the planet Jupiter. He also has a major sign that is associated with addictive disease—the Jupiter/Uranus parallel. In fact, he also has a Jupiter/Uranus/Mars binary eclipse, which is a factor that corresponds well to the planetary dynamics we have already mapped for addictive disorder. The overindulgence that has been part of Harry's life for so many years takes on a new meaning when examined in the light of this powerful binary eclipse.

This exceptionally strong presentation of Jupiter would almost certainly create problems with excess. Both Uranus and Mars embody forceful change and the expression of creative energies. Uranus is also associated with the search for new and inventive creative spiritual principles. Many drug addicts begin their addictive cycle as a part of a spiritual journey with the thought that the drug could potentially open a door that they could not open alone. In Harry's case, work had become his icon and speed was his way of better exploring and communing with his newfound fascination.

In this chart, Jupiter has an index of +600 and Mars has an index of -200. This indicates that the forces represented by Jupiter are so highly unbalanced that they cannot even be checked by the strongly negative Mars index.

Marker Aspects for Addictive Disorder (7)

Conjunctions:
Jupiter/Pluto, Jupiter/Uranus

Sextile:
Jupiter/Neptune

Opposition:
Moon/Uranus

Parallel:
Jupiter/Uranus

Contraparallel:
Mercury/Moon

Planetary eclipse:
Jupiter/Uranus

The GPI for Harry's chart is 22 and the P/N is +1.44.

DAVIS

Davis has been an alcoholic for thirty years. He has been admitted into treatment centers for alcohol detox more than fifty times. He brags that he has never been sober a day in his life. Davis has never held a full-time job, owned a home, or been part of nuclear family since he was kicked out of his family's house at the age of seventeen.

Davis' chart is one of the most active and complex birth charts I have ever analyzed. His birth chart displays a grand elevation of every celestial body except Neptune! Ironically, Neptune is the planet that is traditionally associated with addictions. In addition to his nine grand elevations, Davis has two eclipses (one involving Jupiter) and a Plenary elevation. Furthermore, he has twelve different parallel aspects. A triangle involving Jupiter probably adds to the power of the addictive cycle which has manifested in his life.

Six out of the nine grand elevations in Davis' chart are negative. He has a high order negative karmic index (the sum of the Saturn index and the Mars index). Saturn is considered to be the

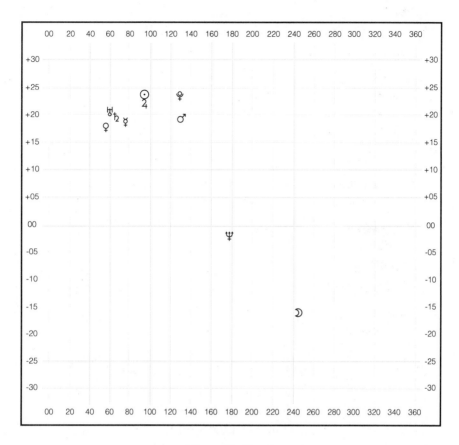

Chart 23: Davis

major malefic in the heavens and is associated with areas where karma and hardship are likely to be the densest. Mars is considered to be the minor malefic, also associated with karma and hardship, but generally to a lesser degree of intensity than Saturn. The karmic index is a measure of the degree of intensity of negative life circumstances (karma) in the birth chart. A high order negative karmic index (more than -18) is associated with extremely difficult life circumstances. This degree of negative energy can only be balanced by a high order positive karmic index (determined by calculating the sum of the major benefics Sun and Jupiter and the minor benefic Venus). We will discuss additional uses of the karmic index in a later chapter.

Marker Aspects for Addictive Disorder (10)

Trines:
    Moon/Pluto, Uranus/Neptune
Sextile:
    Mars/Uranus
Square:
    Sun/Neptune
Oppositions:
    Moon/Uranus, Moon/Venus
Parallel:
    Saturn/Mercury
Contraparallel:
    Moon/Mercury
Eclipse:
    Sun/Jupiter
Grand elevation:
    Pluto (Moon/Pluto trine, Uranus/Pluto sextile,
    Sun/Pluto parallel, Jupiter/Pluto parallel, Triangle ele-
    vation [Sun-Jupiter-Pluto], Exdek Pluto, Proximity
    elevation [Sun/Pluto parallel, Jupiter/Pluto parallel])
The GPI of Davis' chart is 39 and the P/N is -0.625.

High Risk Transits for Addictive Disorder

When the following conditions involving transiting planets occur, persons who exhibit signs of Addictive Disorder can experience an intensification of symptoms.

- Sun/Jupiter sextile
- Jupiter/Neptune sextile
- Sun/Neptune square
- Hidek Mercury
- Jupiter planetary eclipse
- Jupiter/Uranus parallel

Famous Cases

THUS FAR WE HAVE EXAMINED NUMEROUS BIRTH CHARTS THAT HAVE helped to establish that mental illness can be foreseen to some degree in the birth chart. These charts and data have established an identifiable set of marker aspects that point to the potential development of major depression, schizophrenia, addictive disorder, anxiety disorder, and attention deficit hyperactivity disorder.

In this chapter, I will briefly present eight examples of famous people whose life histories suggest a likelihood of mental illness and whose birth charts display, on average, a greater than 246% increase in the number of marker aspects for that particular illness when compared to the control group. The celebrities that I have included in this study are: Princess Diana, Richard Burton, Charles Dickens, Marshall Applewhite, Howard Hughes, Mike Wallace, Howard Unruh, and Edgar Allen Poe.

The birth data for the horoscopes in this study were drawn from established archives, principally the *Lois Rodden DataBank* and the American Federation of Astrologers.

PRINCESS DIANA

Diana, the Princess of Wales, was born July 1, 1961, in Sandringham, England at 7:45 P.M. Diana was one of the most-loved and revered women of modern times. During her lifetime, she was the most photographed woman in the world. Her wedding to Prince Charles was the biggest television event of its kind in history. Her tragic and untimely death saddened the world, and her funeral was watched by more than two billion people.

Diana was the subject of intense media scrutiny and her battles with the royal family were the stuff of many a tabloid article. Her battles with bulimia and depression, as well as her suicide attempts, made international headlines. *Diana: Her True Story* by Andrew Morton chronicles her unhappiness, which began shortly before her wedding day, and reveals a woman trapped in a loveless marriage who eventually sank into the depths of despair.

On one occasion in January 1982, during her first New Year with the royal family, she threatened to take her life. When she was accused of "crying wolf," she hurled herself off the top of a wooden staircase. Fortunately, she was not seriously hurt by the fall, although she did suffer severe bruising around her stomach. Although she was pregnant at the time, mercifully the fetus was not injured. On another occasion she slashed her wrists with a razor blade. Another time she cut herself with the serrated edge of a lemon slicer, and on yet another occasion, during a heated argument with Prince Charles, she cut her chest and thighs with a penknife. She later told friends that these episodes were desperate cries for help.

When she moved to Balmoral, she grew even more melancholy. She became embroiled in tempestuous arguments with the royal family. At a time when she was in the depths of despair, media publicity turned against her as well. Her royal spending sprees and her battles with eating became almost daily news.

Does her birth chart presage major depression? Unfortunately, even though Diana lived in a fairy tale world, her birth chart predicted a substantially higher-than-average astrological predilection for the development of major depression. Diana's birth chart has ten marker aspects for major depression, compared to an average of three for the control group.

The Saturn/Pluto contraparallel and the Saturn/Mercury contraparallel is quite common in the birth charts of individuals who eventually develop depression. In Diana's case, the Saturn/Pluto contraparallel is also further enhanced by a proximity elevation (seventeen minutes). The fact that Saturn and Pluto are both located in the area of high declination adds even more to their potential to astrologically influence the birth chart.

In addition, Diana has multiple negative aspects to the planet Mercury, giving the planet a fifth-degree negative elevation. This degree of negative potential in a planet associated with the conscious mind and rational thought, combined with a negative grand elevation of the planet Mars, may have been instrumental in inciting some of Diana's impulsive and irrational actions. Suicidal thinking combined with multiple suicide attempts would probably be one of the psychological side effects of such a dire planetary interaction.

Diana's chart has a total of four negative grand elevations: Mars, Saturn, Pluto, and the Moon. The planets Jupiter and Neptune also display a fifth-degree negative elevation. This high

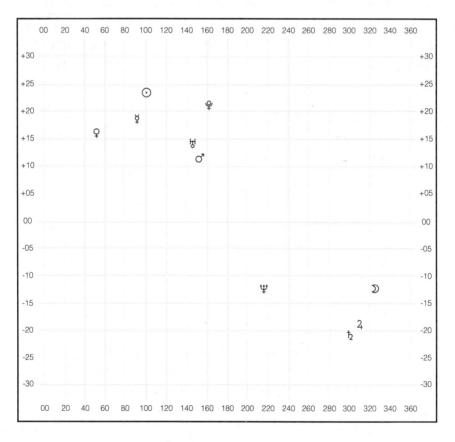

Chart 24: Princess Diana

degree of negative interaction between these four planets is further compounded by the fact that her chart has a very low P/N (-0.41). Her above-average GPI (38) combined with the low P/N and four negative grand elevations (two involving the malefics) would create a tremendous amount of unconscious tension in any person. Diana's unhappy childhood, unfortunate marriage, frequent depressions, suicide attempts, and painfully protracted divorce may have been associated with the effect of the high number of negative planetary interactions in her chart.

On closer examination, we can see that she has an eleventh marker for depression—a Moon-Mars-Uranus triangle hidden within the Moon-Mars-Uranus-Neptune quad elevation. This rare planetary triangle is further enhanced by Neptune, which has well-known associations with the unconscious mind. If one adds this difficult aspect to the rest, a strong tapestry is woven that would suggest that Princess Diana may well have been destined to endure the depression that has become an ironic part of her legend.

Marker Aspects for Depression

Conjunction:
   Sun/Mercury

Contraparallels:
   Jupiter/Mercury, Saturn/Mercury, Saturn/Pluto,
   Pluto/Mercury

Hidek:
   Saturn, Pluto

Proximity elevation:
   Saturn/Pluto contraparallel

Grand elevations:
   1) Pluto (Pluto/Mars conjunction, Jupiter/Pluto con-
      traparallel, Sun/Pluto contraparallel, Saturn/ Pluto
      contraparallel, Hidek Pluto, Proximity elevation
      [Saturn/Pluto contraparallel, Sun-Pluto-Saturn tri-
      angle elevation])

2) Mars (Pluto/Mars conjunction, Mercury/Mars sextile, Moon/ Mars opposition, Mars/Uranus parallel, Neptune/Mars contraparallel, Moon/Mars contraparallel, Quad elevation [Moon-Mars-Uranus-Neptune])

The GPI of Diana's chart is 38 and the P/N is -0.41.

MARSHALL APPLEWHITE

Co-founder of the ill-fated Heaven's Gate cult, Marshall Applewhite is one of the most recent cult leaders to gain posthumous notoriety. His history suggests a long struggle with schizophrenia.

In 1971, Applewhite checked himself into a psychiatric hospital during an episode of depression, auditory hallucinations, and extreme guilt about a series of homosexual affairs. At the hospital, he met a nurse, Bonnie Lu Trousdale Nettles, who would lead him into a new kind of spirituality. Together, they renounced all sexuality, and later Applewhite had himself castrated. They recruited hundreds of followers around the country and required them to dress alike, cut their hair, and repress any sexual identity. They propounded a theology that stated the human body was a mere vessel for an asexual soul, and that it could only find salvation in its home in outer space.

The videotapes of Applewhite's final statements show him to be delusional, sexually repressed, and suffering from a rare case of clinical paranoia, according to a March 29, 1997 *Washington Post* interview with Louis Jolyon West, a professor of psychiatry at the UCLA School of Medicine. Applewhite's life was filled with periods of intense self-recrimination and delusional thinking. The elaborate metaphysical system he and Nettles developed may have arisen as a result of the unique unconscious stresses he endured.

Throughout the two decades in which he led his cult, he assumed names such as Bo, Do, Winnie, and a host of fanciful titles. In their passionate desire to separate themselves from sexuality and their bodies, Applewhite and Nettles interpreted the

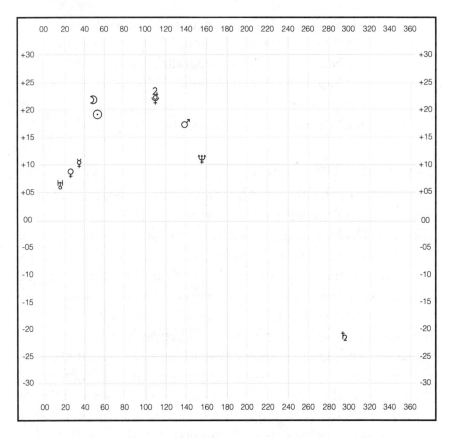

Chart 25: Marshall Applewhite

scriptures to mean that they were going to be martyred and taken up into outer space, there to be bodily resuscitated.

Nettles died in 1985. In 1997, believing the Hale-Bopp comet to be hiding a spaceship that had come for them, thirty-eight Heaven's Gate members died with Applewhite. They packed a bag, swallowed a huge dose of phenobarbital mixed in applesauce, washed it down with vodka, and lay down on their beds to "shed the shell," as they put it. Other cult members ritually covered them in purple cloth, and then took their own lives.

Marshall Applewhite's chart displays six marker aspects indicating a strong propensity for the development of schizophrenia. He has an overabundance of negative planetary energy in the form of five negative grand elevations: Sun, Moon, Jupiter, Saturn, and Pluto. Of these, the Moon, Saturn, and Pluto are high order elevations. In addition, we again see intense planetary tension in the form of a very low negative P/N (-0.34) combined with a high GPI.

Applewhite has two Hidek planetary eclipses and three aspects enhanced by proximity. If one adds the fact that he has four planets (including Saturn) in the Hidek area, we emerge with a picture that is very consistent with that of the test charts we examined earlier.

Applewhite shares a very rare high declination Jupiter/Pluto eclipse with another infamous cult leader—Jim Jones. Their charts are also remarkable in that they display a Jupiter triangle, an elevation also present in the charts of dangerous cult figures Luc Jouret and Jacques Dimambro.

Does this triangle give the native unusual access to the human collective unconscious? Are there other prominent leaders who have displayed preternatural power in this area who also possess a Jupiter Triangle? The answer is a resounding yes! One of the most striking examples of this powerful aspect in the chart of such a person is found in the nativity of a man who led the world into one of the darkest periods in all of human history—Adolf Hitler. Hitler displays a high declination Jupiter Triangle and a Hidek Jupiter/Moon eclipse that is also ominously enhanced by a proximity elevation! This triangle is also shared by one of the most dangerous men alive today—Saddam Hussein. Hussein's birth chart also shows a high declination Jupiter Triangle, further enhanced by a the presence of a Moon/Mars eclipse! Is it mere coincidence that a small number of immensely powerful human beings should share such a rare aspect?

Marker Aspects for Schizophrenia

Trine:
   Moon/Saturn

Square:
   Sun/Mars

Parallel:
> Mercury/Uranus

Hidek:
> Pluto

Grand elevations:
1) Sun (Sun/Saturn trine, Sun/Mars square, Sun/Moon parallel, Sun/Mars parallel, Sun-Moon-Saturn triangle elevation, Sun/Saturn contraparallel, Sun/Neptune square)

2) Moon (Moon/Saturn trine, Moon/Mars square, Sun/Moon parallel, Jupiter/Moon parallel, Pluto/Moon parallel, Saturn/Moon contraparallel, Sun-Moon-Saturn triangle, Jupiter-Saturn-Pluto-Moon quad elevation, Hidek Moon, Saturn/Moon contraparallel proximity elevation, Pluto/Moon parallel proximity elevation)

The GPI for Applewhite's chart is 43 and the P/N is -0.34.

HOWARD HUGHES

Howard Hughes was one of the most enigmatic and mysterious personalities of the last fifty years. He was born in Houston, Texas, and was educated at Rice Institute and California Institute of Technology. At the age of nineteen he inherited the Hughes Tool Company and bought out his relatives to seize full control. Hughes was handsome, tall, smart, dynamic, and he courted starlets by the score. His great love was aviation, and he set a record by flying around the world in ninety-one hours. In 1935 he set a world speed record of 352.4 miles per hour. He built the world's largest plane (the *Spruce Goose)* out of plywood, flew it once, and put it into permanent storage.

Hughes ultimately lost interest in planes, starlets, and films. Even though he was at one time one of the richest men in the world, Hughes probably suffered from a psychotic disorder (clinical paranoia) and possibly severe agoraphobia. His paranoia led him to hold meetings in obscure locations late at night. He began to wear disguises to thwart imagined enemies. Most of all, he dreaded germs. After his 1957 marriage to actress Jean Peters, he insisted on separate quarters to prevent food contamination.

In 1966, he was forced to sell his controlling interest in TWA for $546.5 million. Following this devastating loss, Hughes lived in hotels in Las Vegas, London, the Bahamas, and Latin America. He spent days in the dark endlessly watching the same films—*Ice Station Zebra* was his favorite. He died in 1976, and an autopsy revealed a body shot through with pieces of broken syringes and needles.

There are several positive indicators in Hughes' chart. It displays five positive grand elevations, including a high-order grand

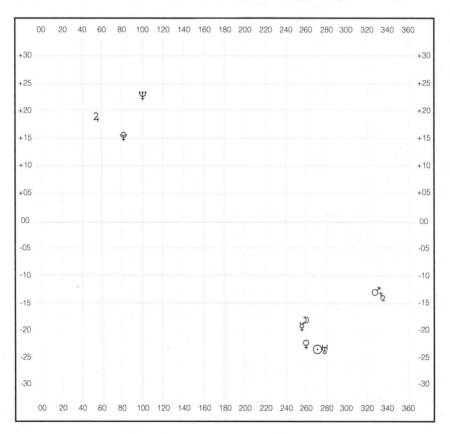

Chart 26: Howard Hughes

elevation of the Sun. He also had a high positive P/N, which generally bodes well for success in life, and a grand elevation of Uranus and Neptune, which may well be associated with his fondness for the unusual, travel, and novel ideas.

Unfortunately, Uranus, the planet that rules eccentrics, is located in the area of extreme declination. More ominously, Howard Hughes' astrological profile suggests that he was highly predisposed to the development of both anxiety disorder and schizophrenia, with five marker aspects for each condition. This double propensity for the development of mental illness probably proved to be overwhelming, even for such a seemingly fortunate chart.

Marker Aspects for Anxiety Disorder (5)

Parallel:
  Venus/Uranus

Contraparallel:
  Sun/Neptune

Hidek:
  Sun

Grand elevations:
  1) Sun (Sun/Uranus conjunction, Sun/Mars sextile, Sun/Venus parallel, Sun/Uranus parallel, Sun/Neptune contraparallel, Quad elevation [Sun-Uranus-Venus-Neptune], Hidek Sun, Proximity elevation [Sun/Uranus parallel])

  2) Venus (Moon/Venus conjunction, Mercury/Venus conjunction, Sun/Venus parallel, Venus/Uranus parallel, Venus/Neptune contraparallel, Quad elevation [Sun-Venus-Uranus-Neptune], Hidek Venus)

Marker Aspects for Schizophrenia

Conjunction:
  Mercury/Venus

Opposition:
    Uranus/Neptune
Parallel:
    Sun/Venus
Hidek:
    Sun
Grand elevation:
    Sun (see above)
The GPI for Hughes' chart is 35 and the P/N is 1.69.

CHARLES DICKENS

Charles Dickens is one of the most popular writers of English literature. He was a masterful storyteller whose keen powers of observation allowed him to create true-to-life characters in tales combining humor, pathos, and social criticism. Dickens was born February 8, 1812, in Portsmouth, England. His most famous works include *David Copperfield, A Christmas Carol, Oliver Twist,* and *A Tale of Two Cities.*

As a boy, he was forced to work in a factory after his father was imprisoned for debt. This experience was to emotionally scar him for the rest of his life, despite the enormous success of his novels. His personal life was overshadowed by a profound sense of unhappiness and incompatibility with his wife. His clinical depression probably contributed to his eventual separation from his wife in 1858, even though the marriage had produced ten children. He died from a stroke on June 9, 1870.

Dickens' birth chart manifests seven marker aspects for clinical depression. It has a total of seven grand elevations. Three are positive (Uranus, Pluto, and the Moon) and four are negative (Jupiter, Mercury, Neptune, and Saturn). He also has one triangle elevation, and one quad elevation. His triangle and quad are both composed of planets that are involved in grand elevations. It is extremely rare that all of the planets in both a triangle and a quad in one individual's chart are involved in grand elevations.

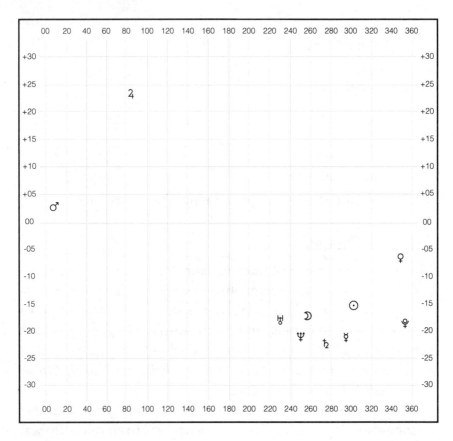

Chart 27: Charles Dickens

The Pluto-Moon-Uranus triangle elevation would greatly enhance Dickens' latent creative potential and may have stimulated his psychic genius. This triangle is common in individuals who have enhanced psychic ability. Dickens was said to carry on conversations with characters from his books. He stated that he could see them and interact with them as if they were real people, and that they often revealed the plot lines of his novels as if they were living out the stories in some parallel world. This may represent some form of clairvoyance that he was able to successfully channel.

Unfortunately, his grand quad elevation is enhanced by a Hidek Saturn, which may account for the particularly bleak, biting social criticism and commentary that permeated his works.

Marker Aspects for Depression

Parallels:
Moon/Uranus, Pluto/Uranus

Contraparallels:
Jupiter/Mercury, Pluto/Mercury, Jupiter/Neptune

Hidek:
Saturn

Grand elevation:
Pluto (Pluto/Venus conjunction, Uranus/Pluto trine, Mercury/Pluto sextile, Moon/Pluto parallel, Pluto/Uranus parallel, Triangle elevation [Pluto-Moon-Uranus], Proximity elevation [Pluto/Uranus parallel])

The GPI of Dickens' chart is 37 and the P/N is .-0.68.

RICHARD BURTON

Born in Pontryhydyfen, Wales, Richard Burton was one of the most talented actors of the twentieth century. He was noted for his Shakespearean stage performances, most memorably his work in *Hamlet, Twelfth Night, The Tempest,* and *Othello.* His most famous films include *Becket* (1964), *Night of the Iguana* (1964), *The Taming of the Shrew* (1967), and *Who's Afraid of Virginia Woolf?* (1966).

Perhaps even more famous than his acting career was his relationship with Elizabeth Taylor. His lifestyle and reported problems with alcohol have also become a large part of his legend. Does he have marker aspects for addictive disease in his birth chart?

Burton's chart reveals that he has a grand elevation of Jupiter, Pluto, and Saturn. He has a total of six elevations that are related to addictive disease. His overall chart dynamics indicate a remarkable amount of balance between the number of positive and negative elevations (P/N = +1.00).

The most prominent indicator of addictive disease among his aspects is the grand elevation and high declination placement of

Pluto. A strong Pluto typically shapes an intense, brooding kind of person, often an introvert. These people often focus on the things that constitute symbols of power in our culture—sex, money, and authority in all its forms. The intense need to manifest power can create complex insecurities and deep, forceful connections with the unconscious mind. This may help to explain Burton's genius for creating such brilliant portrayals of immensely complex characters. The same pressures, when combined with a very strong Jupiter presence (such as his Jupiter triangle and a grand elevation) could lead one to seek huge excesses in the material world—a condition that could also help fuel an addictive personality. This triad of unconscious psychic pressure is an immense burden for any individual.

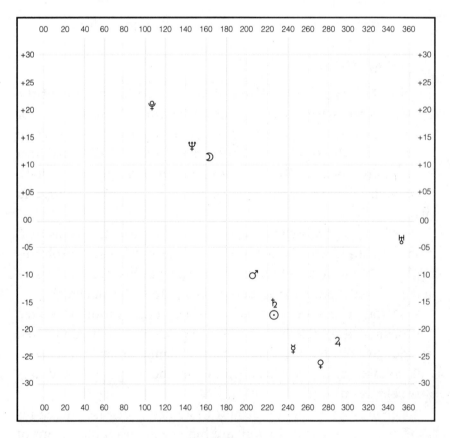

Chart 28: Richard Burton

Marker Aspects for Addictive Disease (6)

Trines:
Saturn/Pluto, Sun/Uranus

Sextiles:
Sun/Jupiter

Squares:
Sun/Neptune

Hidek:
Pluto

Grand elevation:
Pluto (Sun/Pluto trine, Moon/Pluto sextile,
Jupiter/Pluto parallel, Triangle elevation [Jupiter-
Pluto-Mercury], Hidek Pluto, Pluto/Mercury contra-
parallel)

The GPI of Burton's chart is 25 and the P/N is 1.00.

HOWARD UNRUH

Howard Barton Unruh was born and raised in Camden, New Jersey. He was a tank gunner who distinguished himself in battle during World War II, both in the Italian campaign and the Battle of the Bulge. He qualified as a sharpshooter early in his training, and fellow GIs noticed how he would often sit quietly in his barracks fondling his rifle, taking it apart, cleaning it lovingly, and putting it back together. On September 6, 1949, Unruh left his house at 9:00 A.M. In the following hour he shot and killed twelve men, women, and children and wounded four others.

Unruh's case received worldwide attention and shocked the nation with its brutality. He made a statement after the incident that the people had made derogatory remarks about his character. Detective Vince Connelly, one of his arresting officers, asked him, "Are you a psycho?" Unruh answered, "I'm no psycho. I have a good mind." When asked if he was sorry for the murders he had committed, he answered, "I'd have killed a thousand if I'd had bullets enough."[1]

Unruh's diagnosis of schizophrenia has been verified by twenty independent psychiatrists and by his grossly psychotic behavior. He never faced trial, and now permanently resides in the New Jersey State Mental Hospital.

I want to emphasize that most schizophrenics are *not* dangerous or violent people. In this particular instance, however, the psychotic process impelled a very violent, murderous act. In the case of Unruh, his astrological markers clearly lean toward the psychotic illnesses. His profile does not fit the usual high degree of negative elevations and low P/Ns we saw in the earlier charts of schizophrenics. In this case, we may be looking at a completely different type of psychosis—that of a homicidal psychopath. Unruh's reasons for the murders are irrational and paranoid, clear indicators of some form of psychotic disorder.

Unruh has seven marker aspects for schizophrenia in his birth chart. He has a triangle elevation, a quad elevation, four proximity elevations, and three eclipses. The most active planets in his chart are Jupiter, Mercury, and Pluto, which are also the most active planets in the schizophrenia test group. Unruh's chart has a high order negative grand elevation of Jupiter and a high order positive grand elevation of Pluto. This high degree of activity combined with a high complexity index in the chart of a man who is capable of such violent behavior may be related to a psychotic manifestation of a strong unconscious need for power. Similar to the addictive profile, this combination of forces in a highly complex birth may impel the development of an insurmountable torrent of impulses which, if not well channeled, could develop into a delusional system.

Marker Aspects for Schizophrenia

Parallels:
  Moon/Neptune, Sun/Mercury
Contraparallels:
  Sun/Pluto, Mercury/Pluto

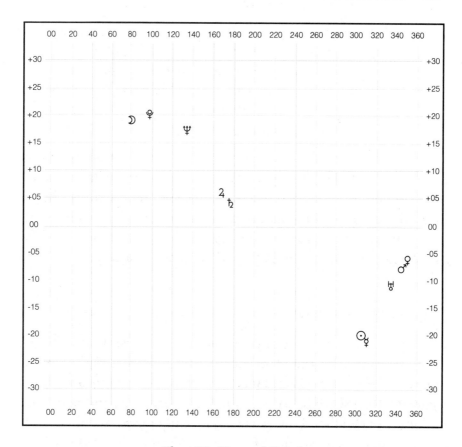

Chart 29: Howard Unruh

Grand elevations:

1) Sun (Sun/Mercury conjunction, Sun/Mercury parallel, Sun/Pluto contraparallel, Sun/Moon contraparallel, Quad elevation [Sun-Pluto-Moon-Mer-
   cury], Proximity elevation [Sun/Pluto
   contraparallel])

2) Moon (Pluto/Moon parallel, Pluto/Neptune paral-
   lel, Sun/Pluto contraparallel, Triangle elevation
   [Pluto-Moon-Neptune], Proximity elevation
   [Pluto/Moon parallel, Sun/Pluto contraparallel])

3) Mercury (Sun/Mercury conjunction, Sun/Mercury parallel, Mercury/Pluto contraparallel, Mercury/Moon contraparallel, Quad elevation: [Sun-Pluto-Moon-Mercury], Hidek Mercury, Proximity elevation [Mercury/Pluto contraparallel])

The GPI for Unruh's chart is 33 and the P/N is 1.063.

Violence in the birth chart has been the subject of numerous astrological studies. To date, however, none of these has included the declinational aspects used extensively in this book. In an upcoming book on the astrological profiles of serial killers and mass murderers, I will present a remarkable series of never-before reported unusual astrological markers that occur in the charts of these people.

Edgar Allen Poe

Edgar Allen Poe was one of the greatest writers ever born. He was the first master of the short-story genre, focusing especially on tales of the mysterious and macabre. Poe was born in Boston on January 19, 1809. His parents were touring actors, and both died in his early childhood. He was subsequently raised by John Allan, a successful businessman of Richmond, Virginia. He was taken to England at the age of six and placed in a private school. He attended the University of Virginia for one year, but in 1827 he was expelled because of excessive drinking and gambling debts. He was also expelled from West Point Academy for missing drills and classes.

Poe apparently suffered from a type of idiosyncratic reaction to alcohol. One glass of sherry could send him on a spree that lasted for weeks. While he was pioneering the mystery story in works like *Murder in the Rue Morgue,* he also indulged in excessive drinking and gambling binges that ultimately brought about his early death.

On October 7, 1849, while on his way home to Richmond, he stopped off in Baltimore and toasted the birthday of a friend. Hours later, he staggered through the streets of Baltimore's red light district in a drunken stupor. It was his last drinking bout. He was found lying unconscious in the street, was rushed to the hospital, and died in the emergency room shortly thereafter.

Some scientists believe that Poe suffered from a brain lesion, which may have affected his behavior. Even if this were the case, there is a wealth of astrological signs in his nativity that would indicate predisposition to a life of addictions. His chart displays twice the number of marker aspects for addictive disease than that of the control group. In addition, Pluto is located only one degree and eighteen minutes from the Hidek position (-19° 42'). This placement would have given him a total of five marker aspects for addictive disease—not that he needed more than double the normal amount in order to manifest an addictive lifestyle.

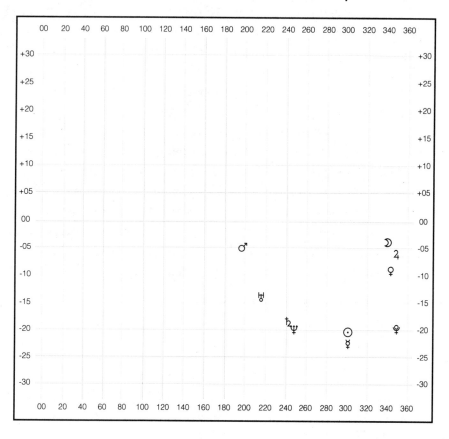

Chart 30: Edgar Allen Poe

At -300, his Mercury index indicates a markedly negative shift from the control group (+170). His +300 Mars index also shows a strongly positive shift upward compared to the controls (-450). He has a fifth-degree positive elevation of Jupiter which includes a Jupiter/Moon planetary eclipse! Furthermore, he has four negative grand elevations involving the planets Saturn, Pluto, Neptune, and the Sun, which contribute strongly to his low P/N (-0.72). He has a single positive grand elevation of the Moon. All of these parameters fit the profile that would have been predicted for that of a person with his life story.

Even though he was a man of impressive brilliance and intelligence, the staggering number of negative elevations that weighed down his chart—combined with the excess of Jupiter, Mercury, and Mars energies—probably empowered the cognitive distortions, excessive spending, and random impulsiveness that marred his life. Once again, we see a low P/N in association with a disabling and ultimately disastrous mental illness.

Poe also had the Saturn/Pluto parallel in his chart. Indeed, part of the impetus for his drinking and gambling may have been an effort to battle a depressive illness. As we have seen in a number of earlier charts, the Saturn/Pluto parallel is a strong predictor for the development of depression. In Poe's case, the Saturn/Pluto parallel is part of a Grand Quad Elevation. This rare configuration may have been a double-edged sword for the master of horror, granting him access to the abysmal and dark regions of the human unconscious while at the same time exposing him to the ravages of a major affective disorder (depression).

Marker Aspects for Addictive Disease

Conjunctions:
  Jupiter/Pluto
Hidek:
  Mercury
Eclipses:
  Jupiter/Moon

Grand elevation:
Pluto (Neptune/Pluto square, Sun/Pluto parallel, Saturn/Pluto parallel, Pluto/Neptune parallel, Quad elevation [Sun-Pluto-Neptune-Saturn], Proximity elevation [Pluto/Neptune parallel])

The GPI for Poe's chart is 31 and the P/N is -0.72.

MIKE WALLACE

Mike Wallace is the ultimate television insider. He is an extraordinarily popular interviewer, well known for his work on *60 Minutes* and *Twentieth Century*.

Wallace's struggle with clinical depression became public knowledge following a libel case in which he and CBS were sued by General Westmoreland. Wallace won the case, but the stress took a severe toll on his health.

In Kathy Cronkite's book *On the Edge of Darkness*, she cites the first sign of Wallace's spiral into depression as his inability to sleep: "...and because I couldn't sleep, I started taking half a sleeping pill, then it went up to one sleeping pill, and then if I wasn't sleeping, I'd take another. And I felt lousy all day long."[2] At Christmastime, in the Caribbean, "I kept looking at the water and thinking, 'Oh boy, that's very tempting.'[3] I think everybody thinks of suicide at one time or another. You get to the point where you say to yourself, 'Hey that would be wonderful. That would kill the pain in a hurry.'"[4]

When Wallace returned from the islands he said, "I was in very, very bad shape. I wound up in the hospital for what we called exhaustion, and I was emotionally and physically exhausted. But really, it was depression. The chief of psychiatry came in and said, 'You're suffering from clinical depression.' I was grateful to have some kind of diagnosis. The mystery was over."[5]

Wallace's birth chart is an excellent study of the astrological markers for depression. Not only does he have twice the number of marker aspects for depression when compared to controls, he also has a high Saturn index (-800) compared to the control group

(-604), a fifth-degree negative elevation of the Sun, and a negative grand elevation of Pluto. His incredibly close placement of Saturn and Pluto (+19° 3' and +19° 6', respectively) places them less than two degrees from the area of high declination. A high declination placement of these two planets would have given Wallace a total of eight marker aspects for depression.

In fact, the entire triangle of Saturn, Pluto, and Neptune is only five minutes apart in Wallace's chart. As I stated in an earlier chapter, parallel aspects of Saturn, Neptune, and Pluto are associated with death and physical injury from all causes. In 1918, the year of Wallace's birth, the world was staggering from a severe global influenza epidemic which claimed the lives of more than

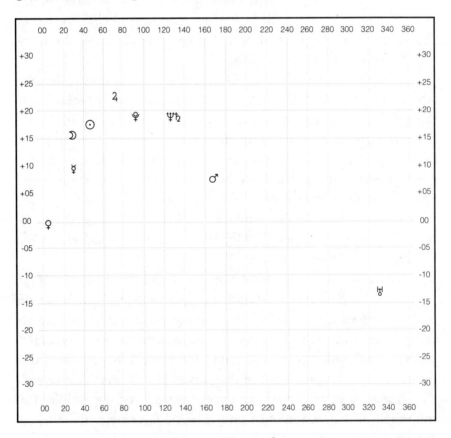

Chart 31: Mike Wallace

twenty million people. Between the years of 1918 and 1920, the proximity of the planets Saturn, Neptune, and Pluto was extremely close, with Saturn and Neptune involved in a planetary eclipse. This placement would greatly exaggerate the effect of this unfortunate celestial event. During the more recent Saturn/Neptune planetary eclipse, the world was plagued by the advent of another even more deadly epidemic: AIDS. During another Saturn/Neptune eclipse, Europe was devastated by the Bubonic Plague and London was destroyed by a disastrous fire that destroyed huge parts of the city. I do not know if Mr. Wallace has suffered from any serious physical injuries or illnesses in addition to his depression, but I have seen this phenomenon repeatedly in the birth charts of patients born with this particular aspect.

The presence of three negative grand elevations, a low negative P/N, and a high Saturn index are all important indicators for potentially intense psychic conflict. The negative energy in this birth chart unfortunately overshadows the energy and intelligence of one of television's most powerful voices. It is a testament to his strength and courage that he has been able to achieve as much with his life and career as he has considering the astrological impediments in his birth chart.

Marker Aspects for Major Depression

Sextiles:
> Moon/Pluto, Moon/Uranus

Parallel:
> Saturn/Pluto

Proximity elevations:
> Saturn/Pluto, Pluto/Neptune

Grand elevation:
> Pluto (Venus/Pluto square, Saturn/Pluto parallel, Sun/ Pluto parallel, Quad elevation [Saturn-Neptune-Pluto-Sun], Proximity elevations [Saturn/Pluto parallel, Pluto/Neptune parallel])

The GPI for Wallace's chart is 27 and the P/N is -0.59.

ENDNOTES

1. J. Robert Nash. *Bloodletters and Badmen*. New York: M. Evans and Company, 1993, pp. 641–644.
2. Kathy Cronkite. *On the Edge of Darkness*. New York: Dell Publishing, 1994, p. 15.
3. Ibid.
4. Ibid.
5. Ibid.

12 Time, Place, and Karma

BEFORE WE FINISH, I'D LIKE TO DIVERGE FROM THE SUBJECT OF MENTAL illness to present two additional important factors in the chart—the temporal index and the karmic index.

In the preceding chapters, we have seen a connection between a low P/N and conflictive life patterns. The P/N is a relative measure of the positive and negative planetary interactions present at the time of a person's birth. Indirectly, I believe this is one way to ascertain some of the inherent characteristics of the temporal environment surrounding a particular event. The temporal environment is equivalent to the soil that an event is planted in. I theorize that the product of the total number of planetary interactions (GPI) and the P/N gives a number that may be used to predict certain characteristics of an event. I also believe that certain planetary indices—in particular, those of Saturn, Mars, Jupiter, Venus, and the Sun—are important in the establishment of a further profile of the characteristics of an event.

The karmic index, like a seed, is a measure of the positive or negative growth potential inherent within a certain event. In examining the birth charts of scores of individuals, I have formed a theory that the planetary interactions at the time of the birth are a useful measure of the positive or negative growth potential within their lives. In other words, a person with a high positive karmic index has an inherently higher potential for growth than a person with a high negative karmic index. Furthermore, a person with a high negative karmic index has a much greater tendency to experience negative and conflictive events within their life spans than people with high positive karmic indices.

These principles were illustrated in the charts in the preceding chapter. Now let's examine a few more remarkable cases that will add further impetus to the theory—the charts of two men, two countries, and two cities.

POPE JOHN PAUL II

Pope John Paul II is one of the most beloved and respected men in the world. His legacy of love, honesty, character, and strength has been the pillar upon which the faith and hope of millions of Catholics have built their devotion to the Church. Despite an assassination attempt and advancing age, he continues to travel around the world while maintaining a rigorous schedule as the

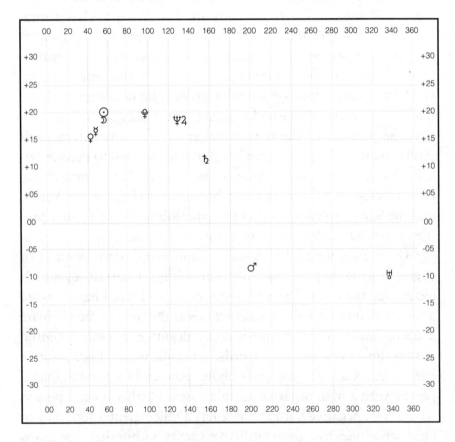

Figure 32: Pope John Paul II

head of the Catholic church. His record of good works, devotion, and love for all is beyond question. His birth chart is a sterling example of an outstandingly positive temporal environment yielding a life that is extremely fertile and prosperous.

Pope John Paul II's birth chart reveals that he was born under excellent conditions. Not only were there six positive grand elevations in the sky, the negative planetary elevations were unusually low in number. Even the complex elevations in his chart—the triangle, plenary elevation, and the eclipses—are positive. His temporal index is three and a half times more positive than that of the control group and his positive karmic index is eleven times higher than that of the control group. Furthermore, his negative karmic index is five times lower than that of the control group. This combination of extraordinarily positive and unusually low negative elevations should, in theory, create an exceptional temporal environment for the growth and development of a very special and very positive life or event. The life of Pope John Paul II is a magnificent testament to one such life.

Outstanding Chart Features: Pope John Paul II

Positive triangle elevation:
    Jupiter/Neptune/Mercury

Positive plenary elevation:
    Sun-Pluto-Neptune-Jupiter-Moon

Planetary eclipse:
    Jupiter/Neptune

Binary eclipse:
    Sun/Moon/Mercury

Positive grand elevations:
    Sun (high order), Moon (high order), Jupiter (high order), Neptune (high order), Mercury, Pluto

Below-average Saturn index:
    -500

Extremely low Mars index:
    -100

Temporal index:
   12,236 (Control: 3,248)

Positive karmic index:
   6440 (Control: 589)

Negative karmic index:
   186 (Control: 908)

The GPI of John Paul's chart is +38 and the P/N is +3.22.

THE MARQUIS DE SADE

Donatien Alphonse Francoise Comte de Sade (the Marquis de Sade) was one of the most cruel and unusual human beings to ever walk the face of the Earth. His very name has become synonymous with pain, and is the root of the term "sadism." His father (Jean-Baptiste Joseph Francoise, Compt de Sade), no stranger to cruelty himself, married a lady-in-waiting in order to seduce the princess she served, then used up both fortune and reputation. His only son, Donatien, was to become an even more lurid figure than his father. His cruelty and debauchery were so notorious that kings burned him in effigy.

At the age of four the young Sade was sent to live with relatives—first his grandmother, then his uncle Abbe de Sade of Ebreuil. He then returned to Paris to attend the Jesuit Lycee Le Grand. It was there that he was first introduced to the whip. At the age of fourteen, he was unleashed upon an unsuspecting puritanical world. By sixteen, he was fighting in the Seven Years War.

In 1763, he married a woman who shared his sense of pleasure, but continued his sexual explorations and affairs. He invited men, women, children—anyone who would help explore his life of pain and lust. One night, his housekeeper, Rose Keller, escaped his attentions by leaping through a window. This act led to one of De Sade's many arrests. He was once jailed for poisoning prostitutes in Marseilles with an aphrodisiac, and again for hiring young children to work as his housekeepers. His mother-in-law eventually had him sealed away in the Bastille, and later in an asylum at Charenton.

He was liberated during the French Revolution, but was by now a broken and penniless man. He then began to write luridly brilliant pornographic works, electrifying tales of depravity that were translated into more than a dozen languages. After he admitted that he had written *Justine,* Napoleon's government sent him back to the asylum at Charenton. While there, he seduced nurses and wrote plays that he directed using inmates as actors.

The Marquis de Sade's birth chart substantiates the theory of the effect of the negative temporal environment. He possesses one of the most negative astrological profiles I have ever analyzed. His negative karmic index alone is nine and a half times lower than that of the control group! That represents a precipitous increase in the number of potential conflicts and hardships that

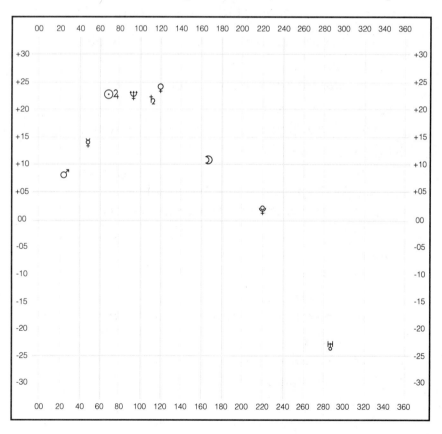

Figure 33: The Marquis de Sade

he would have to endure. His temporal index shows an equally precipitous increase in negativity, and is more than five and a half times more negative than that of the control group. All of the planets involved in the calculation of his positive karmic index have high-order negative grand elevations. Since the measure of the positive karmic index is absolute, its value for his chart is 165% below that of the control group.

When one steps back and analyzes the data in the light of the life story of this man, an astonishing correlation emerges. The negativity of his life very closely matches the negativity evident within his chart. A 946% increase in the negative karmic burden is a monstrous burden for any individual. It would appear that de Sade did live out the life path marked out for him by the planetary patterns etched into space at the time of his birth.

Outstanding Chart Features: The Marquis de Sade

Band elevation:
   Sun/Saturn/Jupiter/Venus/Neptune/Uranus

Negative Hidek elevations:
   Sun, Saturn, Jupiter, Venus, Uranus, Neptune

Negative proximity elevations:
   Venus/Uranus contraparallel, Saturn/Uranus contraparallel, Neptune/ Uranus contraparallel,
   Jupiter/Uranus contraparallel, Sun/Uranus contraparallel

Eclipse:
   Sun/Jupiter eclipse

High order negative grand elevations:
   Sun, Venus, Jupiter, Saturn, Uranus, Neptune

Temporal index:
   -576 (Control +3248)

Positive karmic index:
   +358 (Control +589)

Negative karmic index:
  +8594 (Control +908)
The GPI of de Sade's chart is +45 and the P/N is -0.128.

When one considers the huge contrasts between John Paul and de Sade and the widely divergent nativities from which they emerged, an intriguing question emerges. Does space itself create a pathway along which the events and life patterns of the beings who live within a particular temporal environment are guided? If so, is this guidance applicable only to individuals or does it also apply to larger scale interactions of people: i.e., the life pattern of a country?

THE UNITED STATES

The United States is the most powerful and prosperous country in the world. Its global influence belies its young age and humble beginnings. In the span of just over 200 years, The U.S. has positioned itself as the champion of democracy, and the dollar is one of the most stable and coveted currencies in the world. The technological, intellectual, military, entertainment, sporting, and scientific exports of this country are highly prized commodities. Indeed, U.S. citizenship is a coveted prize. Does the birth chart of the United States presage such a high degree of success and leadership for this young country? Let's take a look.

The birth chart for the United States is exceptionally positive. Its positive karmic index is twenty-two times higher than that of the control group. Its temporal index is more than five times more positive than that of the control group. Its negative karmic index is nearly three times lower than that of the control group. The extraordinarily high number of positive proximity elevations and high order positive grand elevations, combined with an exceptionally positive P/N, certainly make a strong case for the birth of a strong and powerful individual or nation. Indeed, it would almost appear that the founding fathers may have hired an astrologer to map an optimum time for the signing of the Declaration of Independence. If that is the case, I salute the genius and

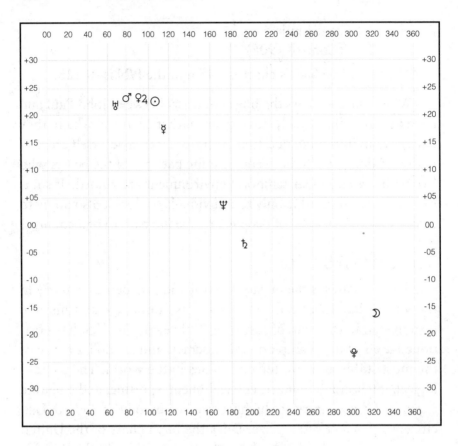

Chart 34: The United States

foresight of this remarkable astrologer. The temporal environment into which the United States was born is exquisite and indicates that it should be a world leader for many centuries to come.

Outstanding Chart Features: The United States

Plenary elevation:
    Sun/Jupiter/Venus/Mars/Pluto

Positive proximity elevations:
    Jupiter/Mars parallel, Pluto/Mars contraparallel,
    Jupiter/Pluto contraparallel, Mars/Venus parallel,
    Sun/Jupiter parallel, Jupiter/Venus parallel,
    Venus/Pluto contraparallel

Positive planetary elevations:
Jupiter/Venus, Sun/Jupiter

Positive grand elevations:
Sun (high order), Venus (high order), Mars (high order), Jupiter (high order), Pluto (high order), Uranus

Temporal index:
+17,072

Positive karmic index:
12,804

Negative karmic index:
335

The GPI for the U. S. chart is +44 and the P/N is +3.88.

SOVIET RUSSIA

The U.S.S.R. was founded in Leningrad (then known as Saint Petersburg) on November 7, 1917, as a confederation of Eastern bloc nations, headed by Russia. The history of Soviet Russia is filled with war, famine, and economic instability.

Civil unrest was also prominent throughout the period. The 1921 Makhnovite Rebellion, the 1921 Kronstadt Mutiny, the 1956 Hungarian Revolution, the 1968 Czechoslovakian uprising, and the 1970 Polish uprising are only a few of the numerous clashes that rocked the government during its reign.

In World War II, Russia suffered the highest number of casualties in the world: 20,127,000, almost twice that of Germany (10,500,000) and more than ten times that of the U.S. (1,194,000)! After the war, bloody purges were instigated by Joseph Stalin. These relocations and mass executions led to the deaths of hundreds of thousands of Russian citizens.

This astrological profile indicates that Soviet Russia was conceived in an extremely negative temporal environment. In fact, its P/N is among the lowest I have ever measured. The negative karmic index indicates a twelvefold increase compared to the control group. The temporal index indicates a 566% increase in negativity when compared to the control group. The positive karmic index displayed a fourfold drop in value when compared to the control group.

These are familiar figures when one recalls our discussion of other negative temporal environments. A country with this kind of high order negative activity would have great difficulty surviving for any great period of time. As such, the U.S.S.R. collapsed in 1991, after which a number of independent republics were established, including modern Russia.

Russia is still struggling to rebuild its infrastructure following the collapse of the Soviet Republic and the fall of the Berlin Wall. Modern Russia was "born" during a Saturn/Neptune eclipse, which also plagued its former chart. Beginning in 1991, the Russian government took decisive steps to liberalize the exchange of

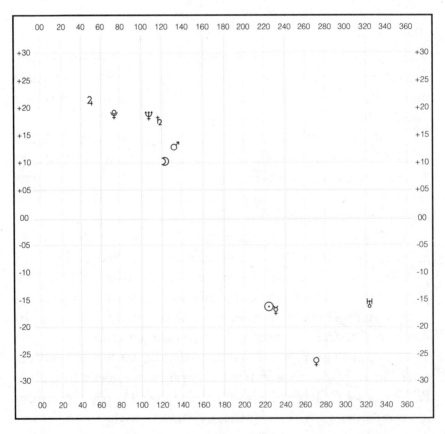

Chart 35: Soviet Russia

its currency, after which the ruble plummeted. In 1992, the ruble's value fell to less than one-hundredth of the U.S. dollar, and in 1993 it dropped to less than one-thousandth of the U.S. dollar. Russia's rulers would do well to think long and hard about the new birth date for their country!

Outstanding Chart Features: Soviet Russia

Negative quad elevations: Sun/Pluto/Neptune/Saturn, Sun/Mercury/Neptune/Saturn, Sun/Mercury/Saturn/Uranus

Negative proximity elevations: Saturn/Mercury parallel, Pluto/Neptune parallel

Negative grand elevations: Sun (high order), Mercury (high order), Saturn (high order), Neptune (high order), Pluto, Uranus

Temporal index: -574

Positive karmic index: +147

Negative karmic index: +10,877

The GPI for Soviet Russia's chart is 39and the P/N is -0.1471.

HIROSHIMA AND NAGASAKI

In a single week in the middle of the twentieth century, more humans died in a war than in any other time in history. Is there any indication that space created a temporal environment for even such an unspeakable act? I speak, of course, of two days that will live in infamy in the annals of war: August 6, 1945, and August 8, 1945. On these two days, the United States dropped atomic bombs on the Japanese cities of Hiroshima and Nagasaki.

Once again, we see the presence of a very negative temporal environment in association with a very negative event. In both instances, the stars themselves seemed to be arranged in such a

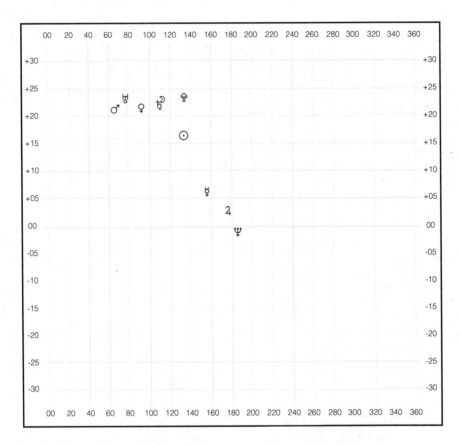

Figure 36: Hiroshima Atomic Explosion

way as to presage some form of mass destruction. Unfortunately, the numbers and the death toll speak for themselves.

Outstanding Chart Features: Hiroshima Atomic Explosion

Negative band elevation (enhanced by high declination):
Moon/Uranus/Mars/Venus/Saturn/Pluto

Negative proximity elevations (parallels):
Venus/Moon, Moon/Uranus, Saturn/Venus,
Venus/Mars

Negative grand elevations:
Moon (high order), Venus (high order), Mars (high order), Saturn (high order), Uranus (high order) Pluto

Temporal index:
  -988

Positive karmic index:
  376

Negative karmic index
  8500

The GPI for Hiroshima's chart is 42 and the P/N is -0.2353.

Outstanding Chart Features: Nagasaki Atomic Explosion

Negative high declination (plenary elevation):
  Venus/Mars/Saturn/Uranus/Pluto

Negative proximity elevations (parallels):
  Venus/Mars, Saturn/Venus, Saturn/Mars

Negative grand elevations:
  Venus (high order), Mars (high order), Saturn (high order), Pluto (high order), Uranus

Eclipses:
  Sun/Moon, Uranus/Mars

Temporal index:
  -1269

Positive karmic index:
  351

Negative karmic index:
  8148

The GPI for Nagasaki's chart is 47 and the P/N is -0.27.

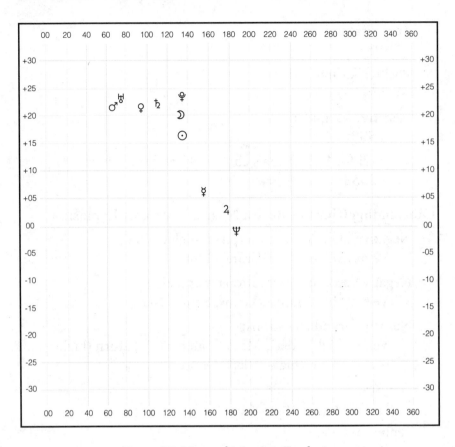

Figure 37: Nagasaki Atomic Explosion

13   The Hidden Order

PRIOR TO COMPLETING THIS RESEARCH, I FELT THAT I HAD DEVELOPED a good understanding of the applications and uses of astrology. However, after examining numerous instances where applying the new techniques outlined in this book have revealed fresh insights, I have cultivated a healthy respect for the work of the ancients and their predictive abilities. The concept of "a time and a place for all things" now takes on a different light.

I believe that the time and place of our birth has a profound influence on the development of mental illness. I do not believe that this influence is explainable by chance or by simple environmental factors. For centuries, many of the greatest scientists and thinkers from all over the world have postulated that there may be a hidden order of influence and intelligence that affects every living thing. This hidden order has been analyzed by some of the greatest minds in physics, astronomy, chemistry, philosophy, and mathematics.

Modern physics has come very close to gaining further insight into this riddle with new discoveries about the bending of space and the probable existence of dark matter. Physicists believe that only a small fraction of the weight of the universe is accounted for by visible matter and that there must be an exceptionally heavy but invisible form of matter that is as yet undiscovered. Scientists also believe that the galaxies and stars are arranged on the fabric of space much like sequins or studs on a garment. Two years after the theory of relativity was published in 1916, Austrian physicists Josef Lense and Hans Thirring concluded that, as a consequence of general relativity, massive bodies spinning in space would drag space and time around like funnel clouds whipping up debris. The 6,700 pound Rossi X-ray Timing Explorer, a satellite designed to measure radiation emanating from the stars, has now provided the first observational evidence of space-bending.

Italian astronomers Luigi Stella and Mario Vietri were the first to recognize the RXTE's potential as a tool in the search for space-time distortion. Using this satellite, they found that gas and space debris orbiting fifteen neutron stars wobbled slightly as it traveled at speeds near 100,000 kilometers per second. The wobble, which they liken to the wobble of a child's top as it slows down, was a telltale sign of space-time distortion. Complex calculations indicated that the only plausible explanation for the dimensions of the wobble was a distortion in space-time.

If space is composed mostly of a dense invisible material that holds the entirety of visible reality in some form of implicit order, what effect would movement of this material have on the universe? If this material can influence the movement of space, does it affect the reality within these areas of movement? And if so, is this effect deliberate and can it be predicted or measured?

Astrologers have attempted to answer the last of these questions with plots and measurements of the movements of the stars and planets. There have been hundreds of instances where competent astrological predictions and guidance have proven uncannily accurate in their prescient discernment of human affairs. However, the work of these astrologers has done little to answer the other half of the question—is this effect deliberate? Does space think? Is there an ordering intelligence behind reality?

In light of the above data, as well as the dozens of cases we have presented in the preceding chapters, I firmly believe that there is some order of intelligent guidance within the fabric of space that influences the course of events in the universe. This force, by means yet unknown, may bend or fold the fabric of space according to some great plan and, in effect, influence the position of the stars and planets.

These shifts in position, which we map in the birth chart, may well be our only way of observing and measuring the effect of this force at this time. It would appear, however, that once this change has occurred in the fabric of space, an intelligent and interactive temporal path is created that may profoundly influence the life forms born in its wake. This may be the intention of the hidden order of intelligence that mediates the workings of the astrological profile. Only time and further research will reveal the veracity of these speculations.

Future Directions

The Signs Project has been envisioned as a continuing study of the uses of the new astrology techniques I have presented in this work. Each project will examine different aspects of the human condition in an attempt to determine if there are recurring marker aspects that are applicable. I will cover a vast array of research topics, including:

- Astrological markers for sainthood
- Astrological markers for future world events and disasters
- Astrological markers for the world's most gifted psychics and healers
- Astrological markers for creative genius
- Astrological markers for mass murderers and serial killers
- Astrological markers for mental illnesses in celebrities and famous people

This list is by no means exhaustive. The new techniques I have pioneered in this research lend themselves to the study of almost any group or special event which might grab a researcher's fancy. I also plan to turn the research outline into a program that could then be used by astrologers at all levels. In this way, I hope to broaden the appeal and use of astrology as a rich, vibrant, and beneficial science, available to all who seek to further their awareness of the universe and their place within it.

Bibliography

Astrology References

Reinhold Ebertin. *Astrological Healing.* New York: Samuel Weiser, 1989

Associated Newspapers Ltd. *The Complete Book Of Fortune.* New York: Crescent Books, 1936

Alex Bethor. "The Astrological Review," (Paris, 1909).

Michel Gauquelin. *Cosmic Influences on Human Behavior.* Santa Fe, N.M.: Aurora Press, 1973.

Sandy Johnson. *The Book of Tibetan Elders.* N.Y., Riverhead Books, 1996

Michael Beazley. *The Compleat Astrologer.* N.Y., McGraw-Hill, 1971

Ariel Guttman and Kenneth Johnson. *Mythic Astrology.* St. Paul, MN, Llewellyn Publications, 1993

Medical References

American Psychiatric Association. *Diagnostic and Statistical Manual of Mental Disorders, Fourth Edition.* Washington, D.C., American Psychiatric Association, 1994

Harold I. Kaplan and Benjamin Sadock. *Comprehensive Textbook of Psychiatry.* N.Y., Williams & Wilkins, 1989

Harold I. Kaplan and Benjamin Sadock. *Handbook of Clinical Psychiatry,* N.Y., Williams & Wilkins, 1990

Jerry Weiner, ed. *Textbook of Child and Adolescent Psychiatry.* Washington, D.C., American Psychiatric Pr., Inc., 1996

Biographical References

Andrew Morton. *Diana: Her True Story*. N.Y., Simon and Schuster, 1997

Carl Posey. *The Big Book of Weirdos*. Phoenix, AZ, Paradox Press, 1995

J. Robert Nash. *Bloodletters and Badmen*. M. Evans and Company, 1993

Kathy Cronkite. *On the Edge of Darkness*. New York, Dell Publishing, 1994

APPENDIX A

CONVERSION CHART FOR PLANETARY POSITIONS

Degree (X Axis)	Sign/Degree
00	0° Aries
20	20° Aries
40	10° Taurus
60	0° Gemini
80	20° Gemini
100	10° Cancer
120	0° Leo
140	20° Leo
160	10° Virgo
180	0° Libra
200	20° Libra
220	10° Scorpio
240	0° Sagittarius
260	20° Sagittarius
280	10° Capricorn
300	0° Aquarius
320	20° Aquarius
340	10° Pisces
360	30° Pisces (0° Aries)

APPENDIX B

WORKSHEET FOR MODERN ASTROLOGY CHARTS

Aspects (longitudinal)

Conjunctions_____

Trines_____

Sextiles_____

Squares_____

Oppositions_____

Longitudinal proximity (within ten degrees)_____

Positive elevations _____

Negative elevations_____

Aspects (declinational)

Parallels_____

Contraparallels_____

Triangle elevations_____

Quad elevations_____

Plenary elevations_____

Band elevations_____

Elevation by high declination_____

Elevation by extreme declination_____

Elevation by proximity_____

Positive elevations_____

Negative elevations_____

Bilevel elevations (combined declination and longitude)

Planetary eclipses (two planets)_____

Binary eclipses (three planets)_____

Plenary eclipses (four or more planets)_____

First degree elevations_____

Second degree elevations_____

Third degree elevations_____

Fourth degree elevations_____

Fifth degree elevations_____

Grand elevations_____

Planetary indices

Sun index_____

Moon index_____

Mercury index_____

Venus index_____

Mars index_____

Jupiter index_____

Saturn index_____

Uranus index_____

Neptune index_____

Pluto index_____

Summary Indices

GPI_____

P/N_____

Temporal Index_____

Positive Karmic Index_____

Temporal Index_____

Complexity Index_____

APPENDIX C

DECLINATIONAL CHART FORM

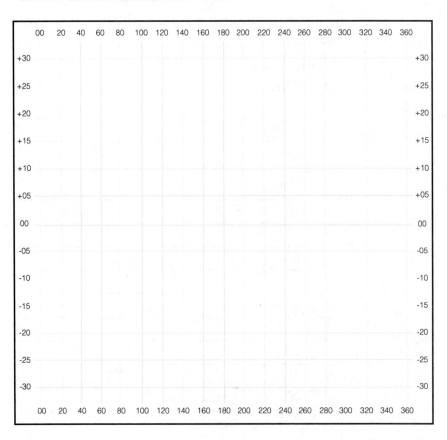

Name:_____

Date:_____

Time:_____

Location:_____

Longitude:_____

Declination:_____

INDEX

A

Adams, Evangeline, 2-3

agoraphobia, 75-77, 82, 85, 87, 148

AIDS, 163

alcohol, 94, 125-126, 131, 138, 153, 158

amphetamine, 126-127

Applewhite, Marshall, 141, 145-148

Aristotle, 10

Arthur, 101-103

atomic bomb, 175

B

Bacon, Francis, 11

Bethor, Alex, 12

Betty, 71-73

Bible, 6

Bode, Liv, 56, 100

Brahe, Tycho, 12

bubonic plague, 163

Burton, Richard, 141, 153-155

C

Cameron, 131-133

Carl, 106-108

Catherine, 87-89

celestial equator, 27, 29, 31, 37-38

cocaine, 109, 126-127, 131-133

CT scan, 93

Cynthia, 68-71

D

Daniel, 82-84

David, 67-68

Davis, 138-140

de Sade, Marquis, 168-171

Denise, 64-66

Diana, Princess, 141-145

Dickens, Charles, 141, 151-153

DSM-IV, xiv, 43, 56-57, 76, 94-95, 110

Dimambro, Jacques, 147

LOOK FOR THE CRESCENT MOON

Llewellyn publishes hundreds of books on your favorite subjects! To get these exciting books, including the ones on the following pages, check your local bookstore or order them directly from Llewellyn.

ORDER BY PHONE

- Call toll-free within the U.S. and Canada, 1-800-THE MOON
- In Minnesota, call (612) 291-1970
- We accept VISA, MasterCard, and American Express

ORDER BY MAIL

- Send the full price of your order (MN residents add 7% sales tax) in U.S. funds, plus postage & handling to:

  Llewellyn Worldwide
  P.O. Box 64383, Dept. K302-6
  St. Paul, MN 55164–0383, U.S.A.

POSTAGE & HANDLING

(For the U.S., Canada, and Mexico)

- $4 for orders $15 and under
- $5 for orders over $15
- No charge for orders over $100

We ship UPS in the continental United States. We ship standard mail to P.O. boxes. Orders shipped to Alaska, Hawaii, The Virgin Islands, and Puerto Rico are sent first-class mail. Orders shipped to Canada and Mexico are sent surface mail.

International orders: Airmail—add freight equal to price of each book to the total price of order, plus $5.00 for each non-book item (audio tapes, etc.).

Surface mail—Add $1.00 per item.

Allow 4–6 weeks for delivery on all orders.
Postage and handling rates subject to change.

DISCOUNTS

We offer a 20% discount to group leaders or agents. You must order a minimum of 5 copies of the same book to get our special quantity price.

FREE CATALOG

Get a free copy of our color catalog, *New Worlds of Mind and Spirit*. Subscribe for just $10.00 in the United States and Canada ($30.00 overseas, airmail). Many bookstores carry *New Worlds*—ask for it!

Visit our website at www.llewellyn.com for more information.

Astrological Timing of Critical Illness
Early Warning Patterns in the Horoscope
NOEL TYL
Foreword by Mitchell Gibson, M.D.
Introduction by Jeffrey Wolf Green

Now, through master astrologer Noel Tyl's work, astrology has a thoroughly tested method with which to understand and anticipate the emergence of critical illness: from the natal horoscope, throughout development, and within the aging process. Astrologers can use Noel Tyl's discovery to work with people to extend life as much as possible, to live a full life, and to do it all with holistic understanding.

Tyl painstakingly researched more than seventy cases to test his patterning discoveries Your analytical skill will be alerted, tested, and sharpened through these very same cases, which include notables such as Carl Sagan (bone cancer), Betty Ford (breast cancer), Larry King (heart attack), Norman Schwarzkopf (prostate cancer), and Mike Wallace (manic depression), and many, many others.

- Explore the predisposition to pathology as indicated in the horoscope

- Learn the aspect patterns natally that, with Solar Arcs and Transits, reveal extreme challenge to the life system, the onset of specific body weakness and critical illness

- Exercise your observational skills and your facility reading planetary networks and timing patterns through the study of 70 horoscopes

- Lead your clients to seek the early medical attention that could save their lives

- Learn to communicate the indications of the horoscope to the client in a sensitive manner

1-56718-738-2, 288 pp., 7 x 10, charts $19.95

Mythic Astrology
Archetypal Powers in the Horoscope
ARIEL GUTTMAN & KENNETH JOHNSON

Here is an entirely new dimension of self-discovery based on understanding the mythic archetypes represented in the astrological birth chart. Myth has always been closely linked with astrology; all our planets are named for the Graeco-Roman deities and derive their interpretative meanings from them. To richly experience the myths which lie at the heart of astrology is to gain a deeper and more spiritual perspective on the art of astrology and on life itself.

Mythic Astrology is unique because it allows the reader to explore the connection between astrology and the spirituality of myth in depth, without the necessity of a background in astrology, anthropology or the classics. This book is an important contribution to the continuing study of mythology as a form of New Age spirituality and is also a reference work of enduring value. Students of mythology, the Goddess, art, history, Jungian psychological symbolism and literature—as well as lovers of astrology—will all enjoy the text and numerous illustrations.

0-87542-248-9, 382 pp., 7 x 10, 100 illus., softcover $17.95

Archetypes of the Zodiac
KATHLEEN BURT

The horoscope is the most unique tool for personal growth you can ever have. Once you understand how the energies within your horoscope manifest, you can then work consciously with it to remove any obstacles to your inner growth.

The technique offered in this book is based upon the incorporation of the esoteric rulers of the signs and the integration of their polar opposites. This technique has been very successful in helping clients or readers modify existing negative energies in a horoscope so as to improve the quality of their lives and the understanding of their psyches.

There is special focus in this huge comprehensive volume on the myths for each sign. Some signs may have as many as four different myths coming from all parts of the world. All are discussed by the author. There is also emphasis on the Jungian Archetypes involved with each sign.

This book has a depth often surprising to the readers of popular astrology books. It has a clarity of expression seldom found in books of the esoteric tradition. It is very easy to understand, even if you know nothing of Jungian philosophy or of mythology. It is intriguing, exciting and very helpful for all levels of astrologers.

0-87542-088-5, 576 pp., 6 x 9, illus., softcover $16.00

Synthesis & Counseling in Astrology
The Professional Manual
NOEL TYL

One of the keys to a vital, comprehensive astrology is the art of synthesis, the capacity to take the parts of our knowledge and combine them into a coherent whole. Many times, the parts may be contradictory (the relationship between Mars and Saturn, for example), but the art of synthesis manages the unification of opposites. Now Noel Tyl presents ways astrological measurements—through creative synthesis—can be used to effectively counsel individuals. Discussion of these complex topics is grounded in concrete examples and in-depth analyses of the 122 horoscopes of celebrities, politicians, and private clients.

Tyl's objective in providing this vitally important material was to present everything he has learned and practiced over his distinguished career to provide a useful source to astrologers. He has succeeded in creating a landmark text destined to become a classic reference for professional astrologers.

1-56718-734-X, 924 pp., 7 x 10, 115 charts, softcover $29.95

Twelve faces of Saturn
Your Guardian Angel Planet
BIL TIERNEY

Astrological Saturn. It's usually associated with personal limitations, material obstacles, psychological roadblocks and restriction. We observe Saturn's symbolism in our natal chart with anxiety, while intellectually proclaiming its higher purpose as our "wise teacher."

But now it's time to throw out the portrait of the creepy looking, scythe-wielding Saturn of centuries ago. Bil Tierney offers a refreshing new picture of a this planet as friend, not foe. Saturn is actually key to liberating us from a life handicapped by lack of clear self definition. It is indispensable to psychological maturity and material stability—it is your guardian angel planet.

Explore Saturn from the perspective of your natal sign and house. Uncover another layer of Saturnian themes at work in Saturn's aspects. Look at Saturn through each element and modality, as well as through astronomy, mythology and metaphysics.

1-56718-711-0, 6 x 9, 360 pp.   **$16.95**

The Ultimate Cure
The Healing Energy Within You
DR. JIM DREAVER

The Ultimate Cure will open a door into consciousness and literally bring you into a direct, first-hand experience of illumination—an experience that will stimulate your mind, warm your heart and feed your soul.

Dr. Jim Dreaver provides a first-hand account of the spiritual journey and outlines the steps needed to live in the world with an authentic sense of wisdom, love and power. He addresses the issues of meditation, work as a spiritual exercise, harnessing the power of the mind, conscious breathing, and healing the wounds of the past. Dr. Dreaver's main theme is that spiritual presence, which is the source of all healing, is an actual, palpable reality that can be felt and tapped into.

To realize enlightenment, you must have a tremendous hunger for it. This delightfully honest and wonderfully human book will stimulate your appetite and, by the time you turn to the last page, will leave you feeling totally satisfied.

1-56718-244-5, 6 x 9, 288 pp., softcover $14.95

For the readers of

Signs of Mental Illness
Only:
A FREE Natal Chart Offer!

Thank you for purchasing *Signs of Mental Illness*. As you will see in this book, there are a number of ways to construct a chart. The easiest way, of course, is by computer, and that's why we are giving you this one-time offer of a free natal chart. Once you receive your chart from us, *Signs of Mental Illness* will provide you with everything you need to know to analyze it according to Dr. Gibson's ground-breaking method! Complete this form with your accurate birth data and mail it to us today. And enjoy your adventure in discovery through astrology!

Do not photocopy this form. Only this original will be accepted.

Please Print

Full name_____

Mailing Address_____

City, State, Zip _____

Birthdate: Month_____ Day_____ Year_____

Birth time_____ ❑ A.M. ❑ P.M. (If unknown, use 12:00 P.M.)

Birth place: City_____County_____

State _____ Country_____

Check your birth certificate for the most accurate information!

Complete and mail this form to:
Llewellyn Publications Special Chart Offer
P.O. Box 64383-K302-6, St. Paul, MN 55164
Allow 4-6 weeks for delivery.